SECOND FIDDLE

Please pass round.
enter name below!

Ray Phillips.

By the same author:

With All Thy Mind
One Man's Testimony
Pacific Pilgrimage
New Guinea News
History of the London Missionary Society 1895-1945
Christian Missions and Social Ferment
The Local Church
Christian Ambassador: a life of A.L. Warnshuis
The Ecumenical Movement
Ecumenical Progress

SECOND FIDDLE

Recollections and Reflections

NORMAN GOODALL

London
SPCK

First published 1979
SPCK
Holy Trinity Church
Marylebone Road
London NW1 4DU

ACKNOWLEDGEMENTS

Thanks are due to the following
for permission to quote from
copyright sources:

The Tablet Publishing Co:
'Roman Pilgrimage', *The Tablet*,
10 and 17 September 1977.

Mrs C.B. Brink: Paper delivered
by Dominie C.B. Brink to the
1953 Conference of the Dutch
Reformed Churches held in
Pretoria.

Printed in Great Britain by
Billing & Sons Limited
Guildford, London, and Worcester

ISBN 0 281 03675 6

CONTENTS

I, being in the way,
the Lord led me . . .

Genesis 24. 27

The orchestra, mainly composed of Oxford amateurs who played with the Bach Choir, was rehearsing Verdi's *Requiem*. Not for the only time, some of the players were achieving effects not anticipated by Verdi. After one such variation the conductor — Sir Hugh Allen — with an agonized shout stopped the proceedings and pointedly addressed one of the second violins. 'You!', he cried, 'go back to bar so-and-so and play it alone.' The result was what he (and I) expected. I muffed it and the great man dropped his baton and said 'Hell!'. Yet I was allowed to continue playing with the orchestra.

This book is not about music. But it *is* about playing a part with fellow performers in an unfinished symphony. Sometimes, as the following chapters will show, I have been entrusted with responsibilities of a leading kind. Often I have found greatest satisfaction in playing a secondary role. There have been glorious harmonies and agonizing discords and I know what it feels like to muff the notes and depart from the composer's intention. But I have been allowed to play with the orchestra for a long time and I want to say 'thank you' for the privilege. This is my main intention in writing this book.

Each chapter refers to people as well as the movements and organizations with which I have been associated. I hope it will be apparent that my delight in friendship and my gratitude to friends is a dominant theme of the book. In addition to the many I have named there are far more whom I have not named. To all, named or unnamed, I offer these pages — especially to my wife, the 'real doctor Goodall', and our beloved family.

In the process of writing I have relied greatly on the encouragement and criticism of some busy people who have found time to read the manuscript in whole or in part. Chief amongst these have been Max Warren of dear memory, Dr F.W. Dillistone, Dr Kenneth Slack, Dr John Huxtable, and Bishop George Appleton. Of special timeliness has been the encouragement and help of Dr Donald Coggan, Archbishop of Canterbury. How *he* has found time equal to his generous goodwill I can scarcely imagine. For repeated typing of the manuscript and the preparation of the index I record my gratitude once again to Miss Verleigh G. Cant.

Benson, Oxford   NORMAN GOODALL
March 1979

1 MADE IN BIRMINGHAM

It was not surprising that my school-fellows envied me. I lived in a sweet-shop. They were wrong, however, in assuming that I could eat all I wanted. We had our disciplines, laid down by my father and kept as a matter of course. On Saturdays we could serve ourselves one generous pennyworth and at other times there was a special box in which were kept the 'seconds'. These were chocolates which had served their time in the window display and had lost their first freshness, though not their succulence. 'Seconds' were not to be sold; they constituted a family reserve. The ration was one for each of us at bedtime, with a greater freedom on Sunday evenings during the intervals of the family sing-song. There was another box marked 'bits'. Into this were thrown squashed chocolate creams, jellies that were now mushy, boiled sweets which had lost their hardness and become candied. The result was a glutinous mass, very tasty to the discerning. Several local urchins knew of this speciality and for a halfpenny they could buy a generous serving of stickiness. One customer was never charged even a ha'penny for his portion: this was the road-sweeper, adult in years but still a child in mental development. I can see his eager face as he leaned over the counter and, like one sharing a delicious secret, would ask in a whisper 'Got any bits?'

The discipline in the matter of helping ourselves was no doubt good for us but I fancy it was also necessary if the narrow profit margin was not to be eaten away. We were a large family. I came twelfth in a succession of thirteen children. Five of my brothers and sisters I never knew; long before I was born they had died within the first years or months of their fragile existence. In 1895, the year preceding my birth, the recorded mortality rate in Birmingham of children under five years was 95·6 per thousand. Our family far exceeded this average. It often seemed strange to me that there had been brothers and sisters whom I never even met. Occasionally there would turn up amongst the family oddments

1

an old photograph of our mother nursing a baby. We used to speculate about the baby's name. None of us could identify it. Only mother knew, and she never forgot.

My own first acquaintance with death came when I was about ten years old. Of my four brothers the eldest came and went intermittently. I was half afraid of him and yet eager for his visits. The fear came from his sombre bearing. There was a curious and pathetic dullness about the eyes. The happiness in his company was largely due to his ear for music. He had begun to learn the piano but was too impatient to continue lessons. He could, however, play by ear almost any melody that had attracted him and we loved him when he was in a jovial mood and 'rattled the ivories'. I remember his return from the Boer war when I was five or six years old. As I look at his enlistment and discharge papers which I still possess I can recapture the feel and smell of his uniform and my early wonderment at the huge ostrich egg which he brought home as a souvenir. He had enlisted for three years but after eighteen months was discharged as an epileptic. It was this that made him something of a stranger amongst us. He would manage to secure work in various parts of the country only to lose his job as soon as his malady was discovered. As often as not he would then come home, bandaged and sullen, waiting for a chance to start again. He was in his twenty-sixth year when news came that he had died in bed, suffocated as a consequence of his last epileptic fit. I know I missed this elusive brother, but I also recall a curious feeling of excitement during that dramatic day when we talked to one another about the news of his passing. I overheard scraps of sad conversation between mother and father, including their sorrow that we could not afford the kind of burial they would have wished. It was during one of the many periods of hardship when the shop was doing badly, so brother Will was buried in what was then called a 'common grave'. For some months afterwards one or other of us would visit the gloomy cemetery to see if our family name had yet been added to the scores of others on the one huge stone. When at last we were satisfied that he was named with the penurious dead we ceased to visit the cemetery.

The shop and the rooms behind and above were the source of most of life's joys as well as the place of our initiation into some of its sorrows. During the whole of my boyhood nine or ten of us lived 'over the shop'. I still cannot understand how we managed, or rather how our beloved parents managed. A bathroom was unheard of. Behind the shop was a small sitting-room and a kitchen. There was a tiny yard about 10 ft by 15 ft, with a lavatory in one corner and a little washhouse in the other. We doubled and trebled up in the bedrooms. My three sisters shared an attic lighted from the roof by a fan-light. Until we left school mother made nearly all the boys' clothes; sailor suits were the main pattern. Father regularly repaired the boots of the entire family. The shop was open from eight in the morning until midnight. Father was fastidious about cleanliness, and being an accomplished amateur joiner made all the shop fittings himself. From early years jobs were allotted to each of the children. I used to deliver ginger beer in a home-made handcart and I can see in my mind's eye some of the tradesmen's entrances where, if I was lucky, a kindly cook would reward me with a cake or a biscuit. A tiny corner of the shop was partitioned off to constitute the 'office'. There was just room for one person at a time to stand there and it was in this office that I was first allowed to handle invoices and record the day's takings.

It is not only fond recollection which causes me to place my father and mother amongst the greatest as well as dearest people I have ever known. Father had no schooling. His own father was an amiable drunkard and one of my father's earliest tasks in life was to do the round of a number of public houses late on Saturday night and to guide him home. Yet this grandfather of mine, whom I never met, cared that his son should at least learn his letters so a local barber was paid twopence a week to teach him to read. By the time he was eight years old he was already a wage-earner, first as a boy doing odd jobs in a sweet factory and later at the bench in one of Tangye's engineering shops. In his teens he was a member of a gang which acquired a considerable reputation for its skill in breaking up political meetings. The main venue was in the great Bingley Hall, Birmingham, in which such orators as Bright and Cobden held forth. The body of the hall was without seats; the hearers stood massed before the plat-form. One or other party would engage my father's gang when the cause could best be served by a rumpus. Father, being slightly built and very lithe, would at a given signal be hoisted on to somebody's shoulders; he would then leap across the heads of the crowd, jump on the platform and try to upset the chairman's table. This was usually enough to set the ball rolling. It was with three members of this gang that on one boring Sunday night father stopped outside what was then called Wesley Chapel on Constitution Hill, Birmingham. Something was going on inside the Chapel and the boys decided to go in and create a disturbance. Shortly afterwards three of them slunk out and disappeared. Father remained and experienced a sound conversion in the authentic Methodist tradition. From this point onwards the Christian faith and the Church — or rather the Chapel — meant everything to him and was a source of the best gifts which he subsequently shared with his family. There was never any doubt about the authority of this religious experience, or of its continuing potency. It remains an astonishment to me that he was held within the fellowship of that 'Old Wesley', as the chapel was familiarly known, at such a time and in his circumstances. He was politically a radical and, for good reasons, something of a social rebel, and even after his confession of faith and reception into the membership of the Church he was allowed to occupy only the 'poor' seats. In accordance with custom he was enrolled in one of the Class Meetings which were part of the Methodist discipline, and his class leader was a wealthy industrialist, conservative in politics. This was in a day when the gulf between master and man was abysmal, yet father's loyalty to the Chapel remained unswerving even when he could let himself go in criticism of what he knew to be its fundamental inconsistencies.

There can seldom have been a more profitable investment than the twopence a week spent on teaching my father his 'letters'. It purchased a key into a universe of delight for himself, his children, and children's children. As soon as the boy of six began to read nothing could stop him. He rummaged in the penny boxes of the second-hand bookstalls and picked up anything that looked good. In his young manhood history and biography became his happiest hunting ground. I still possess a four-volume edition of Macaulay's *History of England* for which he paid fourpence. He delighted also in what was generally classified as belles-lettres; the art of the essay fascinated him — Macaulay, Emerson, Lamb, Hazlitt, and such later practitioners as Birrell, Chesterton, Lynd, E.V. Lucas, 'Alpha of the Plough'. I still wonder what it was in his background or in himself which gave a certain fastidiousness to his choice. He could feel the difference between good writing and the cheaper varieties. There was an odd consequence of this against which I was inclined to rebel in my childhood. I could bring home the *Boy's Own Paper,* the *Captain* or *Chums*, but the *Magnet* and *Marvel* were banned. This had nothing to do with their contents. Questions of obscenity or corruption were scarcely on the horizon. The objection was solely one of style. Contributors to the *Boy's Own Paper* and *Captain* wrote in the tradition of Talbot Baines Reed and G.A. Henty. Their school and adventure stories were the work of recognized craftsmen in the world of letters, but Greyfriars of the *Magnet* and Sexton Blake of the *Marvel* were the product of pulp writers and father was convinced that at a time when the formation of taste mattered greatly my discriminating powers would be endangered by confusing the two genres, so while I could laugh aloud with him over the fat boy in *Pickwick* my chuckles at the gluttony of Billy Bunter had to be kept in check.

For those who had never seen the inside of a school John Cassell, the Strand tea-merchant, was one of the greatest benefactors. Self-educated, he went into publishing with a reformer's zeal for the helping of others. In 1850 he launched the *Working Man's Friend*, an 'improving' magazine with pictures and simple letter-press. Two years later he followed this with the *Popular Educator*, a penny magazine which had been running for about ten years when my father bought his first copy and began systematically to work through its weekly courses. Years later these beneficent helps to the self-educated were marvellously reinforced by such editions as Nelson's sixpenny classics (beautiful little cloth-bound volumes), Cassell's sevenpenny modern novels and that epoch-making enterprise of Dent's — the shilling Everyman's Library. Long before I thought of reading their contents I knew which shelf housed J.R. Green's *Short History of the English People*, Motley's *Dutch Republic*, Gibbon's *Decline and Fall*, and White's *Natural History of Selborne*. Some of these volumes, bought at their original price of sixpence, or a shilling, are still among my best-loved possessions.

My own schooling was mainly confined to what were then known as 'council schools', which taught to a sixth or seventh standard up to the age of fourteen. Schooling beyond that age was not in sight for me. There was a moment when I could have gone to a grammar school on a scholarship but acceptance of this was finally ruled out simply on the ground that it was essential for me to begin earning as soon as I was legally free to leave school. We were never on the poverty line but the fear of poverty was real and it never occurred to me that any other course should or could take precedence over helping to ease the financial strain on the family. In later years when most of us had found our own way in life, two brothers and I had the satisfaction of providing a home in modest comfort for the beloved parents. Even so, father's total savings at his death amounted to around £20. During the last two of my school years I enjoyed some kind of promotion. The council school was selecting a few boys for transfer to what was classified as a 'higher grade' school. Father was eager that I should take advantage of this even though it involved a school fee of sixpence a week and a capital outlay of a shilling for the school cap. The curriculum differed only slightly from that of the council school, the main variation being that some elementary French was taught. I enjoyed the change, partly because of one or two admirable teachers and also for the fun of becoming 'boss's monitor' during my last year. There was no such post as that of head of school, but it was the practice of the headmaster to appoint whoever happened to be top boy in the seventh standard as his private monitor. This meant little more than being a part-time office boy but whenever the headmaster — a formidable martinet — looked in at my classroom and beckoned me for some errand I would leave the class with an enormous feeling of self-importance, enhanced by some good-humoured quip from my teacher about gentlemen-in-waiting or his majesty's private secretary. The distinction was all the more enjoyable because the headmaster paid an honorarium of a shilling a month.

While day school ended at fourteen, evening classes provided rich compensation. For four years after leaving school I spent three or four evenings a week at the local technical school taking courses in English, maths, book-keeping and accountancy, shorthand, commercial law, and a curious course in professional jargon called 'commercial correspondence'. This programme made for fairly long days. I would leave home before eight o'clock in the morning for my work in a city office, walking the four miles to save tram fare. I would then return home around six o'clock and spend from seven until ten in the evening at the technical school. It was an exceedingly happy period. The social life of 'The Tech' was lively and I took full advantage of its many opportunities for music-making.

Music as well as books meant much to us at home though many of my earliest delights in it were of a very unsophisticated kind. Street musicians were plentiful. Some, I realized, were pretty awful but there were one or two groups which gave us unalloyed pleasure. One of these was a harp, violin, and clarinet trio. The players were a shabby, unprepossessing lot and one of them wore a black patch over one eye, but they played well and had an extensive repertoire and father used to encourage them with extra pennies to spend longer outside our shop than at their other stands in the village. Another source of musical delight was provided by the annual Trades Exhibitions in the Bingley Hall, Birmingham, where for several weeks one or other of the German and Austrian bands which roamed the country in those days would give daily performances. We had season tickets to the Exhibitions, chiefly for the purpose of attending these promenade concerts.

My greatest fortune musically came when I was seven years old. Father had learned that a young woman violinist was in need of a room in which to receive pupils. He offered the use of our 'parlour' without charge and in return the violinist offered free lessons to one of the family. I was the lucky beneficiary. A generous uncle passed on to me a half-sized fiddle which he had kept since childhood and this was the beginning of years of delight. I never reached any considerable standard as a player but I had a passport to pleasure and my adorable young teacher was an authentic musician who kindled and nourished a passionate devotion to music in others. She secured for me a place amongst the second violins in a local amateur orchestra, mainly on the ground that I would be

7

useful to the adult players by putting up and taking down the music stands before and after rehearsal. I now have no idea of the competence of the orchestra but I cannot hear certain overtures — *Ruy Blas, Oberon, Merry Wives of Windsor* — and certain Beethoven and Schubert symphonies without remembering my introduction to them from a second fiddle desk. I also owe to the violin something more than music. My wife has told me that it was the violin which awakened her reluctant interest in me as a possible boyfriend. In this I got the better of the bargain for, as pianist and singer, she was a better musician than I and I fell for her contralto voice, cool, clear, and beautifully disciplined. It is an unfailing source of happiness to us that children and grandchildren have maintained the musical succession and far outstripped us both.

Not long after his conversion Wesley's Chapel was the scene of another transforming experience for my father. This also had immeasurable consequences for others. One Sunday evening he noticed a young girl without a hymn book. After some hesitation he moved near to her and offered to share his book with her. At the close of the service he asked if he might accompany her home. On the way he learned a little about her. She was a servant girl, over-worked and badly treated. A few months later she accepted his offer to share the rest of life with her and for more than fifty years they were all in all to one another. Memories rooted in the deepest affections tend, I suppose, to gain in fragrance as the decades pass but neither I nor any other member of my family can recall a moment when our thoughts of this dear woman were other than those of wondering love and undying gratitude. Her formal education was as negligible as my father's. Throughout her life reading was a task she found difficult. Apart from the Bible I only once caught her with another book. It was Kingsley's *Water Babies*. Writing was a still more arduous undertaking. I never received a letter from her through long periods of absence from home and the only scrap of her writing I have ever seen is a scarcely legible signature which I persuaded her to write in a book which I valued. Yet her instinct for beauty in colour and sound, and especially in the daily courtesies was impeccable. It may seem strange but the picture of her which I carry in my mind's eye is not that of a smiling face. I remember her smile and I can recall a gentle laugh, but such a word as 'merry' is not one which I would instinctively apply to her. Her dear face was serious, not infrequently tinged with sadness. What made it unforgettable was a profound and moving beauty deriving from an infinite tenderness and caring. She was a toiler all her life. There was a moment at the end of her days when a brother and I were looking at her hands, lined and worn with the years of labour in the service of those she loved. Touching one of her hands my brother said, 'They remind me of the words "I bear in my body the marks of the Lord Jesus".' He was right. In the whole realm of human relationships I have known no love greater than hers.

'I think we can employ you, but you look very young.' So said the rather dour chief clerk of the South Staffordshire Water Works Company, after having put me through whatever tests seemed appropriate for a new office-boy. 'I expect I shall grow out of that, sir,' I said, and he grunted 'All right. Start next Monday. The pay will be eight shillings a week.' So I learned how to keep a postage-book and to tie up huge parcels of water-rate demand notes for distribution to the various area collectors. I even learned — after much travail — how to operate the heavy wet copying press without smudging the letters. Many of these were still hand-written in copying ink. Before long I was promoted to the rank of junior clerk and for some months I wrote demand notes for water rates addressed to all the inhabitants of Kingswinford. Doing nothing but this from nine to five began to pall and I was thankful when the end of the first quarter arrived and I could report to the chief clerk for fresh instructions. 'What do I do now, sir?', I inquired. 'Begin on the next quarter's', he said.

I have always been blessed by the encouragement and goodwill of older men, at any rate until I became old enough to realize that it was my turn to repay encouragement with encouragement. In the South Staffordshire Water Works Company there was an old rate-collector who, amongst his other duties, was custodian of the register of stocks and shares. He also inscribed the share certificates in a copper-plate hand. As a relief from the tedium of writing demand notes I had eventually been allowed to work as a supplementary typist, female typists being unheard of in those days, and this good man condescended to dictate to me. He was a perfectionist in the setting out of a letter — the right margins, the right centring of the type on the page, the gradations of protocol in 'Sir', 'Dear Sir', 'Dear Mr', 'Your Lordship' . . . and he was especially finicky about the number of lines occupied by the legend

10

I have the honour to be,
    Sir,
        Your obedient Servant.

One other particularity of his I came to appreciate, though I
fear that in later years it caused me to drive some of my own
typists to tears. He regarded it as a betrayal to send out a
letter on which there had been even the slightest erasure.
Rubbing out, however neatly done, was unpardonable; the
faulty letter must be scrapped and a fresh start made.

In the course of this apprenticeship my kind disciplinarian
said, 'If you want to get on you should get out of here.
There's no future in it for such as you. You should try to get
on to the staff of the Birmingham City Treasurer. Write to
the Deputy Treasurer; he's the coming man, and if you could
get under his wing you'd be made.' So I wrote, in as near
copper-plate as I could contrive, on foolscap paper and with
appropriate margins, to the Deputy City Treasurer — one
Arthur Collins — solemnly affirming that

I have the honour to be,
    Sir,
        Your obedient Servant.

The letter, to my delight, produced a reply. There was no
vacancy in the City Treasurer's office but the great man would
give me an interview on a certain date. In due course I presented myself and was ushered into Mr Collins's room. He
was writing, and without looking up from his desk said, 'Sit
down, Goodall,' and continued his writing. The minutes went
by — three, five, seven — and no sound but that of his pen
and no glance in my direction. At last he looked up, picked
up from his desk the day's *Times* (a journal which I had never
before handled), threw it across to me and said, 'Read aloud
the first leader'. I did my best and the only comment was 'I'll
take you to one of my senior clerks. He will find out what
you are like at figures.' A few days later I received another
letter offering me an appointment at twelve shillings and sixpence a week, following which I exchanged the writing of
demand notes for the writing of cheques to be signed by no
less person than the City Treasurer himself — a remote and
incommunicable deity who never spoke a word as I stood

11

beside his desk with blotting-paper at the ready as he put his signature on cheque after cheque.

Arthur Collins was indeed a coming man at that date. Succeeding to the City Treasurership and the Presidency of the Institute of Municipal Treasurers and Accountants and other professional honours, he was much sought after in financial circles generally and especially in the area of municipal finance. His staff regarded him with mingled admiration and fear. He had style, a certain panache, and expected from others the kind of hard work on which he himself throve. It was an exciting discipline to be even a very junior member of his staff.

Early in 1915, though a little under what was then military age, I succeeded in enlisting in the Royal Army Medical Corps. Conscription had not yet been introduced. We were responding to the famous Kitchener poster with its minatory finger and 'Your King and Country Need You'. I once saw that great moustache and the monumental figure attached to it when the legend took flesh and inspected our battalion. My two years in the army did little, I fear, towards vanquishing England's foes. I spent a year route-marching around the villages of Essex. We did a twenty-mile march every Monday, Wednesday and Friday, and occasionally on Tuesdays and Thursdays we received some crude instruction in first aid from a foul-mouthed and dirty-minded sergeant. My unit was commonly referred to as 'The Lost Ambulance', though we were found for a few weeks in the village of Banbury where some of us were entrusted with minor ward duties in an improvised hospital which had been set up in the village hall. Patients were few. There was little work for us and on night duty we occupied spare beds in one of the wards and slept in comfort, except for one nightmare night. On this occasion we had a real patient who gave promise of becoming obstreperous. Just after midnight he threw some kind of fit which none of us was capable of diagnosing or treating with knowledge. However, we had noticed that the little dispensary contained, oddly enough, a jar of leeches. We knew this to be a classical remedy for certain excited conditions so we spent a long time trying to persuade the little beasts to fasten on to a good thing. We succeeded at last but I was revolted by the way in which they then fattened as they feasted. Mercifully, the more gorged they became the quieter became the patient and when they fell off satiated the poor man sank into a well-earned sleep. But it is a horrid business trying to put satisfied leeches back into their bottle.

After such heroics for king and country I managed to get transferred to the Artists' Rifles, a regiment of whose history and reputation I stood somewhat in awe. My new companions were as mixed as the old ones, but they included some representatives of worlds which I had not entered. There was a staff members of *Punch* who was a mainstay of its 'Charivaria' and who wrote humorous verse under the pseudonym of 'Dum-Dum'. There was a memorable moment in the canteen when someone struck a chord on the piano and John Goss held us spellbound with the voice that later became world famous. There was a genial comrade named Parker who for many years was secretary to the D'Oyly Carte Opera Company, and I marched alongside a congenial musician who wrote one of the best-selling ballads of that period, 'Somewhere a voice is calling'. But in relation to the real business of winning the war I have to acknowledge that I could add nothing to the laurels of a regiment whose motto was *Cum Marte Minerva*, in spite of the fluke by which I became classified as a first-class shot and earned an extra sixpence a day for the distinction. I have never liked guns and on the rifle-range at Rainham, where we went for our final tests, lying prone in the mud, a distant target half obscured by marsh mist, I found it better to close my eyes at the moment of pulling the trigger, with the fortuitous result that I got a record number of bull's-eyes. In truth, however, despite a lasting admiration, even through my pacifist years, for the really disciplined and dedicated Service man, I can only recall with humiliation that as a soldier I was a dead loss to the cause. I became medically classified as 'C2' instead of 'A1' and was never in the van on the assault course. I failed to acquire that peculiar twist of the bayonet which is intended to play havoc with the entrails of its victim, and I maddened my instructors by the lack of conviction with which I plunged the steel into my dummy enemy, uninspired by the lofty injunction to 'Rip him up, damn you!'. Eventually Authority, reluctantly subscribing to the doctrine that the pen is mightier than the sword — which didn't promise much in certain

13

hopeless cases — decided to use my skill as a shorthand writer. I then spent many hours trotting around the parade ground after a quick-tempered colonel who, assuming that he who runs may write as well as read, dictated to me chunks of what I believe became part of 'The Times' *History of the War*. On occasion he also dictated letters to his son at Eton in a style which suggested that he himself had been brought up on Lord Chesterfield's *Letters to His Son*.

From this somewhat uncivil service I was seconded towards the end of 1916 to the Civil Service and here I came again under the kindly wing of Arthur Collins who in the meantime had been lent by the City of Birmingham to the Ministry of Munitions as a financial adviser. A few weeks later, just as I was leaving the Ministry one evening, Collins handed me a letter and said: 'Take this to St Ermin's Hotel in Westminster. See the hotel manager and tell him that you are to be given possession of the hotel. You are the first member of the staff of the Department of National Service. The hotel has been commandeered by the Office of Works and the residents are beginning to move out. I shall be joining you there before long and Neville Chamberlain will arrive as soon as he can free himself from Birmingham.'

I then remembered that a few days earlier Lloyd George, as Prime Minister, had announced that Neville Chamberlain, Lord Mayor of Birmingham, had been appointed Director-General of National Service with responsibility for surveying the relative manpower needs of industry and the Services, adjudicating between rival claims and determining which civil employments should be regarded as reserved occupations. This was at a time when, following the end of Asquith's government, there was a widespread clamour fostered by Lloyd George for 'business government'. Neville Chamberlain seemed to fit the new image to perfection. He had business experience plus a deservedly high reputation in local government, though it had been assumed by many in Birmingham that he had no wish to emulate the political career of either his father, the meteoric Joseph, or his half-brother, the stolid Austen. In fact, the manner in which he accepted this first post in national administration suggested a reluctant acquiescence in an unwelcome summons rather than an eager response to a congenial vocation. Lloyd George in his memoirs was later to say of this appointment that 'it was not one of my successful selections'. In comparison with some of his other references to Chamberlain this must have been one of Lloyd George's rare understatements. Chamberlain, though less free with his opinions, found no kindred spirit in Lloyd George. In fact he developed a distrust of the Prime Minister and a resentment against him which continued for the rest of his days and contributed to the bitterness of exchanges between the two men all through Chamberlain's later parliamentary career. The brief year in which he tried to make something of his Director-Generalship in the Department of National Service was clearly an unhappy one. Whatever personal factors contributed to the disillusionment, much of the trouble lay in the imprecise character of his assignment, especially in its bearing upon the existing authority of the Service Departments and the Ministry of Labour. Further, Chamberlain was only the head of a Department, not a Minister directly responsible to Parliament. He had no seat in the House of Commons. On his resignation Lloyd George turned the Department into a Ministry and replaced the Director-General with a Minister of National Service who embarked on his task with the encouragement of a knighthood, a seat in the House of Commons and a Privy Councillorship. The new Minister was Auckland Geddes, a former Principal of McGill University and Professor of Anatomy. When Lloyd George commandeered him to succeed Chamberlain, Geddes was a temporary Brigadier-General and Director of Recruiting at the War Office. His subsequent rise in office was swift. By 1920, little more than three years after his first entry into Parliament in the interests of business government, he had held the posts of Minister of National Service, President of the Local Government Board, Minister of Reconstruction, President of the Board of Trade, and British Ambassador to the United States.

Auckland Geddes was a brother of Eric Geddes of 'Geddes Axe' fame, one of the Government's early post-war economy drives. He too came into politics on the wave of this same passion for business government. In appearance he was more of the tycoon than his brother and was obviously a man of immense drive. He became for a short time the First Lord of the Admiralty, Minister of Transport, and a member of the Imperial War Cabinet. I had dealings with both the Geddes

15

brothers from my junior post but the contacts, though always pleasant enough, were brief and official.

I had reason to work more closely with two other men who, from this much-maligned Department and Ministry of National Service, went on to high parliamentary office. When he left his General's uniform in the War Office and assumed civilian attire before entering the new Ministry of National Service, Auckland Geddes brought with him a young barrister, one of his staff lieutenants. This was Philip Lloyd-Graeme, who became a joint secretary of the Ministry. I remember him as being very confident, as well as competent, with an easy charm and a clear determination to get on. He entered Parliament in 1918 and subsequently held office as President of the Board of Trade, Secretary of State for the Colonies, Secretary of State for Air, Minister for Civil Aviation, and Secretary of State for Commonwealth Relations. In the process he had changed his name from Philip Lloyd-Graeme to Philip Cunliffe-Lister in 1924 and from 1935 until his death in 1972 he was known as Viscount Swinton. He was an influential member of the Conservative Party and in his later years was greatly respected as a senior statesman. R.A. Butler regarded him as a man of Prime Minister calibre.

The other of these two men was one of Neville Chamberlain's early choices for his staff. This was a Glasgow barrister named Robert Horne whom Chamberlain appointed as head of his Agriculture Department. Horne often enlivened my office with his good humour and general ebullience. Lord Beaverbrook later described him as 'smooth and friendly . . . a competent Parliamentarian given to Scottish dialect stories — often twice-told'. He also entered Parliament in 1918 and within the next five years had held office as President of the Board of Trade, Minister of Labour, and Chancellor of the Exchequer.

My own modest niche in this war-time Department and Ministry was first as private secretary to Arthur Collins whom Chamberlain had appointed as Secretary of the Department. At this time Collins's reputation as a financial pundit was growing rapidly; alongside his demanding new tasks he continued to engage in a good deal of private practice as a financial adviser to municipalities. This was a role mainly required when municipal boundaries were being changed or when corporations were taking over responsibilities hitherto carried by statutory companies such as water and gas companies. After long days in the National Service Department I would spend some hours each evening devilling for Collins in this private professional work of his. My most vivid recollection of this side-line was in connection with the financial clauses of a bill on which Collins had been briefed as expert witness. One evening, expecting a few hours unusual leisure I was asked by Collins to stay on to work with him in the final compilation of figures which he needed before appearing on this case at the House of Lords next morning. So we settled down to work again in the office until nearly midnight when we adjourned to Collins's flat in Whitehall Court. Here we continued working together until four o'clock next morning, at which point Collins decided to get a few hours sleep. The remaining calculations were of a fairly routine character and I was left to finish them. At six o'clock in the morning I was able to put the completed work on my chief's desk and I went out to my lodgings at Finsbury Park deciding to have a morning in bed before returning to Westminster. After a troubled sleep in which I was haunted by nightmare columns of figures which refused to balance I woke up to learn from an attendant doctor that I was suffering from diphtheria. My kind and patient hostess had looked in to wake me and being troubled by my appearance had sent for the family physician.

When I returned to the office some weeks later Collins rewarded me with a new opportunity. The Department of National Service was to be provided with a Parliamentary Secretary. Would I like to be his private secretary and so enjoy a further type of experience which might prove useful when I eventually returned to the City Treasurer's office in Birmingham? Behind this appointment of a Parliamentary Secretary there lay part of the reason for Neville Chamberlain's frustration in his task. It was not only that he was unable to answer for himself in the House of Commons. There was no one else directly responsible for dealing with the Department's affairs before Parliament. For a time we were mainly represented by Arthur Henderson, then Minister without Portfolio, but Henderson's position and other responsibilities gave him no inside knowledge of what was happening in the new Department and this was at a time when Chamberlain and all his works were under fire both in Parliament and press. My own dealings with the Director-General were only occasional, except for his first few weeks at St Ermin's when I acted as his private secretary pending the appointment of a senior civil servant to the post. During this time I found Neville Chamberlain, as Sir Arthur Salter later described him, 'courteous without geniality', but on one occasion even the courtesy vanished when I reported to him a telephone message which I had received from Lord Northcliffe's secretary. This was to the effect that this all too powerful and dangerous press lord had seen, without any right to do so, the draft of a circular which the Department proposed to issue. His Lordship wanted Mr Chamberlain to know that unless the circular was altered at certain points the Harmsworth press would make sure that public opinion was even more thoroughly aroused against the Department and its Director-General. Chamberlain angrily told me to give Northcliffe's secretary a dusty answer. I did so, with the result that next day a slow procession of 'sandwich-men' paraded in front of St Ermin's with placards announcing 'Muddle and Mystery in St Ermin's'.

The new Parliamentary Secretary whom I was to serve was Stephen Walsh, who was then Labour member for the Ince division of Lancashire. He was one of that outstanding group of Labour leaders who entered Parliament in 1906 and constituted for the Liberal Party, even on the eve of its greatest period, a warning of things to come. Walsh was little in stature, and rugged in appearance, and bore the marks of the hard way which he had trodden towards leadership. He had become a working miner at the age of thirteen. In one of his reminiscent moments he told me that at one time he and Harry Lauder were working in the same pit and, while the men were waiting for a decision from their leaders on whether or not to strike, Harry Lauder kept his mates in good humour all night with his songs and patter. Walsh was a man of great integrity, universally respected and a joy to work with, both through his natural courtesy and in his no-nonsense attitude to office and protocol. He was, I believe, only the second Labour member to be appointed to Government office, Arthur Henderson being the first. Although owing his appointment to Lloyd George as head of the

Coalition Government, Walsh maintained a distant and critical view of his mercurial chief. After a short time in the National Service Department he was transferred to the Local Government Board as Parliamentary Secretary and later in the first Labour Government he became Secretary of State for War.

Walsh's successor as Parliamentary Secretary to what had become the National Service Ministry was (later Sir) Cecil Beck who had also entered Parliament in 1906 as a Liberal, though he later represented Saffron Walden for twelve years as an Independent. His background and inclinations made him more at home in Asquithian Liberalism than within the political ethos of a wartime Coalition Government but I think Lloyd George fascinated him and he followed the Prime Minister's lead with a good-tempered loyalty. Somehow politically he never fulfilled his friends' expectations, and years later his political independence curiously and sadly led him to join the Bottomley group, that small group which unwisely trusted its fortunes to that great 'con' man, Horatio Bottomley. I was saddened to learn of the death of Cecil Beck at the early age of fifty. To me he was uniformly kind and generous and I handled a good deal of his private and constituency correspondence as well as his official letters. This called for some art in drafting the kind of letters which I thought would be fairly characteristic of him in his dealings with all sorts of people. It became something of a game between us to discover whether he would need to alter any draft of mine before signing it as his own composition. In a letter which I had from him some years later he wrote:

What an interesting job we had, full of crises and overwork but still with many occasions for the exhibition of our wit. We really were in the middle of great affairs. Also I think we did secure fair play for a large number of our fellow-countrymen. Your excellent share in all this is never forgotten by me.

It was in this parliamentary work that I became indebted to another of those older men who blessed me with their confidence and encouragement at successive stages of my varied course. Soon after I entered into occupation of St Ermin's Hotel a senior civil servant was seconded to us from the Local Government Board to help in the organization of the new office on civil service lines. This was A.N.C. Shelley, who worked hard to give to an improvised wartime department some recognizable features of the authentic Whitehall tradition. Shelley had a fastidious mind and cared greatly for precision in thought and language. He was proud of the civil service and especially of its influential role in the government of a country where the subtle relationship between the legislature and the executive is of such vital importance. It has always been something of an astonishment to me that such a man should have taken so kindly to the junior who greeted his arrival and did his best to explain why, despite appearances to the contrary, he was the original member of the Department's staff. Shelley had traversed the very correct road in his chosen career — public school, Oxford, the Bar and the old first division of the civil service — and he was a stickler for official good form. It would not have been surprising if he had regarded a bit contemptuously his raw young colleague whose place in the civil service — by no means an unenviable one at that time — had been reached by an unorthodox route. He proved, however, to be one of the most generous as well as skilful guides and I learned from him a great deal more about civil service procedure than how and when to write 'Passed to you, please'. Long after our ways had separated he sent me a note of interest and encouragement headed 'On an anniversary of our first meeting'.

The most fascinating part of my parliamentary work with both Walsh and Beck was the preparation of replies to parliamentary questions. This was often a complicated procedure and it had to be pursued at speed. Data and advice would need to be collected from sundry departments of the Ministry, and successive drafts of the reply tried out. The style had to be one which could epitomize a good deal of information in a few lines, if this were expedient. Or it must try to carry conviction where a certain degree of elusiveness was necessary. The final draft had to be accompanied by a background paper setting out as succinctly as possible the kind of information which the Parliamentary Secretary might require in dealing with supplementaries. All this was done under great pressure but it was an enjoyable exercise.

Not the least of Shelley's services to me was to introduce me to other private secretaries to Ministers or Parliamentary

Secretaries. I would meet some of them in the official gallery of the House, and the handling of parliamentary questions frequently called for some collaboration between us. Amongst these interesting colleagues one of the most genial was J.C.C. Davidson, at that time private secretary to Bonar Law. He became a Member of Parliament and something of an *éminence grise* in the corridors of power, and he was a close friend and confidant of Stanley Baldwin who, at that time (1917–18), was Financial Secretary to the Treasury. While Baldwin was greatly esteemed and regarded as likely to become increasingly influential there was then little expectation of his becoming Prime Minister. Another member who seemed still less likely to reach the highest office was Ramsay MacDonald, one of the least popular men in the war-time Parliament. His role in the early days of the Independent Labour Party, his ultra-radical speeches, and especially his pacifism, produced for many the image of a dangerous and even sinister enemy of society. He was a pertinacious questioner, very skilful in supplementaries, and I always trembled for my chiefs, especially Cecil Beck, when as often happened the Order Paper showed questions from Ramsay MacDonald about the conduct of the National Service Ministry.

MacDonald's rivals in nuisance value to harassed ministers were a redoubtable pair named Pringle and Hogge, Opposition Liberals during the Lloyd George Coalition Government. Question time was their finest hour. They were adroit Parliamentarians with a diabolical skill in framing supplementaries designed to produce spluttering answers which could make the best-informed minister sound like a defaulting schoolboy.

I was extraordinarily fortunate in having this glimpse of Parliament during such years as 1917–18. Asquith was leading the Opposition, flanked by other survivors of the great 1906 Government — McKenna, Runciman, and Birrell. Lloyd George was Prime Minister, Bonar Law Chancellor of the Exchequer, Balfour Foreign Secretary, Churchill Minister of Munitions, and E.S. Montagu India Secretary. In the light of later history my good fortune now seems all the greater in that I saw the old Irish Party in its full strength in the House of Commons. John Redmond was still at the height of his powers. John Dillon, Joseph Devlin, and Laurence Ginnell could be heard almost daily, and this remarkable company provided moments both of great hilarity and deadly seriousness, not infrequently touched with nobility. On one of my last occasions in the House I witnessed one of many melancholy chapters in the long tragic struggle to 'settle the Irish question'. Perhaps this is to claim too much for the episode for I was left wondering whether in fact it had been precipitated by a genuine desire to produce a settlement. Two measures were announced simultaneously by Lloyd George. One was designed to bring into operation some parts of the Home Rule Bill which had been suspended on the outbreak of war; the other proposed an extension of conscription to Ireland. The conjunction of the two was bound to produce the kind of debate which would kill both projects, and it did. It was then that I heard Edward Carson speak. In his most withering and contemptuous tones he rang the death-knell of the two proposals and ended with the words, 'They were lovely and pleasant in their lives and in death they were not divided'.

I have naturally wondered whether I might have become a permanent civil servant. I do not know whether this would have become practicable in view of the unorthodox road by which I had become a temporary one. In a generous moment Cecil Beck told me that his friend Freddy had offered to put my name forward for a clerkship in the Treasury. 'Freddy' was the Hon. F.E. Guest, a son of Lord Wimborne and Chief Whip in the Coalition Government. Beck, while holding his Parliamentary Secretaryship, was also a Junior Whip and Vice-Chamberlain of the Household. He hunted closely with Guest, politically and socially. When he asked me whether he should accept Guest's offer I could not, for a medley of reasons, immediately reach a decision. Arthur Collins was expecting my return to Birmingham as his personal assistant, and another possibility, very different from either of these openings, was beginning to disturb me. It therefore came about that in 1919 with the greatest goodwill and understanding of generous minded chiefs from whom I had learned so much and through whom I had been given so many exciting opportunities, I said good-bye to municipal and civil service and began to tread a new and unexpected road into another world of friendship, opportunity, and privilege.

3 SERVANT OF THE WORD

Wesley Chapel, Birmingham, was the setting of the great event to which our family owed everything. There was also another chapel in Birmingham where something happened which indirectly laid upon me a lifelong debt of gratitude. In 1826, seventy years before I was born, one Timothy East, the minister of Ebenezer Congregational chapel in Steelhouse Lane, was asked by a member of his congregation, 'What shall I do with my property? How may I employ it for the honour of God?' The inquirer was George Storer Mansfield, whose sisters Elizabeth Mansfield and Sarah Glover were equally concerned about the future of the family estate. Timothy East's advice resulted in the establishment in 1838 of a theological college for the training of Congregational ministers. This became known as Spring Hill College, Birmingham, and forty-eight years later it was transferred to Oxford where it continues its work as Mansfield College. Since 1919 I have missed only one of the annual commemoration services held in the College Chapel and this one absence was due to my responsibilities overseas. The high point in the commemoration service comes when the long roll of 'founders, benefactors, teachers and administrators' is read. It begins with what now sounds in my ears as a kind of drum roll to a solemn melody — 'George Storer Mansfield, Elizabeth Mansfield, Sarah Glover . . .' Year by year at the sound of these names my sense of the past and my gratitude to it are unfailingly renewed.

My admission to Mansfield was by a road somewhat out of the ordinary. The College was a postgraduate one and up to this point no one had been admitted to read theology without having a degree in some other discipline. This qualification was far from being mine; I had not even taken 'matric', a school examination then below the level of 'A' levels. By one of those coincidences for which 'chance' has always seemed an inadequate word I found myself reading for the Oxford Honours School of Theology as a Mansfield student in 1919.

Until my Army service it had never occurred to me that the Christian ministry might become my vocation. I had been nurtured in a home in which Christian convictions and a warm devotion to the Church powerfully contributed to the happiness of our family life. I had taken it for granted that service to others was at least as important as getting on in the world. But the ministry was outside the range of any professional ambitions I possessed. As with many others of my generation, the ugly tragedy of war brought a new dimension into my thinking. My Army service had been less than useful to the country but it provided me with a further education of the kind which few other schools could have given. Life in the sweet-shop had not been insulated from the life around it. The street was one of my playgrounds. We knew the more notorious drunks by name and sight and the Aston of my schooldays enjoyed its full share of Brummagen characters. Office life enlarged my contact with all sorts of people, but Army life did this with a bluntness and frankness which I had not previously met. It would now be unthinkable that I could reach the age of seventeen without having even heard of venereal diseases and their source. But this was so, and my first lesson in the subject came from a youth with whom I was marching whose gonorrhoea had just been diagnosed. His description of the symptoms and the occasion of his contracting the disease was not muted. On my first night away from home after enlisting, in the billets to which we were allotted I shared a bed (not merely a bedroom) with a costermonger who brought a bottle of stout and a fried herring to bed with him as a late-night snack. This man proved to be one of my most good-natured and generous-hearted fellow soldiers, even though I drew the line at the offer of a bite of his herring. These enlightening contacts did not immediately relate to my vocational decision, though they contributed to a delayed-action awareness of how some people live. What raised more disturbing questions about my way of life was the daily evidence that so many of my own generation were paying the price of death or maiming for responding to the country's appeal. Three or four young colleagues in the City Treasurer's office, friends at adjoining desks, were killed within a few months of our enlisting. I could not be glad that I had escaped this. I was much more humiliated by the gift of further life,

and as the carnage went on I felt burdened beyond bearing
by what I could only feel was a debt of honour. It was within
this upheaval that the girl I had set my heart on – Doris
Stanton – played her distinctive part. As a medical student at
Birmingham University she had become a member of the
Student Christian Movement and the Student Volunteer Missionary Union. Her faith and experience brought a further
dimension to my own Christian life and in this total context
I began to think more searchingly about the nature of those
human needs which can only be met by grace, and I saw my
own vocational disturbance in relation to this. Late in 1918
I had managed to return to the Army. Oddly enough, at this
stage I found it far more difficult to get into the Army again
than many men were finding it to get out. This was due to
the nature of my secondment to the civil service. But friends
in the corridors of power assisted my re-enlistment. One of
the farewells I received from the Civil Service came from
J.C.C. Davidson, who phoned me from the Prime Minister's
office where he was then working. 'What's this about your
going back to the Army? Try not to be a damn-fool, but if
you must, good luck to you!' So I once again became a
private soldier and was under orders for France when the
Armistice was signed and the order cancelled. So my effort
to be brave was again futile. But the short period in barracks
once more had included a memorable evening when, puzzled
and wondering about the future, I spent a long time alone in
the hut which had served as a chapel. At the end of it I knew
that if the way opened towards the ministry I would have to
follow it, though the last thing I felt capable of was public
speaking. I was also acutely aware of my educational defi-
ciencies. I therefore decided that when the war was over I
would resume evening classes and private study in the hope
that I might eventually take a London University Arts degree
as an external student and then apply for admission to Mansfield College to read theology. This plan would also have
provided time in which, with the help of others, there might be
some testing of my vocation. The scheme was defeated by the
coincidence to which I have referred. Early in 1919 I was
finally demobilized. I had already paid some visits to the
Mansfield House Settlement in Canning Town, London, a
centre of social work established by the College. While spending

a few days in London after demobilization, I received word through the Warden of the Settlement (Norman Hyde) that Dr Selbie, the Principal of Mansfield College, was 'somewhere in London' at that time. Could I track him down and tell him of my hopes? I therefore went to Memorial Hall, near Ludgate Circus which housed the offices of what was then the Congregational Union of England and Wales. Just inside the building there was a bookshop and I asked a pleasant-looking assistant if she had any idea where I might discover the whereabouts of one Dr Selbie. 'There he is,' she answered, pointing to a browsing customer in the shop. It was some time before I plucked up courage to approach the great man but at last I did so and stammered something about advice. An hour later I had received and accepted it. My own plan would take too long to accomplish, said Selbie. Could I for the next six months manage to live on a part-time job which would allow me more time for study? 'Learn some Greek and Latin. Read your Bible. Practise essay writing.' I might then sit an entrance examination to Mansfield in June. If the results were satisfactory, said Selbie, he would include me in the few exceptions which the College was making to its normal postgraduate requirements and I could spend three years working for a degree in Oxford. So it turned out. My eventual third class in the Honours School of Theology was a bit inglorious but I suppose it might have been worse in the light of the slender academic equipment which I took to Oxford. My subsequent D.Phil. at Oxford came more than thirty years later. A mere three years university residence with no arts or science degree leaves enormous gaps in knowledge and in the discipline of learning. It implies very shaky intellectual foundations for a profession which is first and foremost concerned with the most fundamental questions. I try to guard against the sin of envy but I have found it difficult to suppress a certain wistfulness as I have watched others taking the more normal five to seven years university work, often including a term at a German, French, or American university, prior to their ordination. And when I think of the fourteen years' training which some of my Jesuit friends have undergone I feel intellectually naked.

It has been the more impossible to avoid such reflections as these because Mansfield College, like its Spring Hill predecessor, is an expression of that Puritan conviction concerning the necessity for a learned as well as godly ministry in the service of the greatest cause of all. Although the Spring Hill College was founded later than the famous dissenting academies of the eighteenth century, it was established on principles as intellectually rigorous as those earlier institutions which challenged the lethargy of the ancient universities and added new dimensions to the meaning of education. When the resources of Spring Hill were transferred to Oxford the College was welcomed in its new home because of the strength of the academic tradition in which it stood, as well as on account of the acknowledged eminence in theological circles of its first principal, Andrew Martin Fairbairn, and the first chairman of its council, R.W. Dale of Birmingham. Among those through whose influence the move to Oxford was made were Benjamin Jowett of Balliol, Edwin Hatch of Christ Church, T.H. Green, the philosopher, and James Bryce, the historian and diplomat. Gladstone, the Grand Old Man and pillar of the established Church, encouraged the move as being beneficent to Oxford as well as to the Nonconformist cause. Adolf Harnack of Berlin hailed the opening of the College as 'an event of historic importance', and a shower of greetings on its inaugural day (18 October 1889) came from Yale, Harvard, Princeton, and Union Seminary, New York, as well as from English, Scottish, and other European universities.

When I entered Mansfield in 1919 the faculty included three scholars of international repute. These were George Buchanan Gray, James Vernon Bartlet, and C.H. Dodd. Dodd was the junior member of this trio, but was already known as one whose scholarship and brilliance as a teacher would set him amongst the greatest of biblical interpreters. The beautiful lucidity of his mind, speech, and pen has been a joy to all who have learned from him. Every new instance of his erudition and perceptive interpretation left me breathless with astonishment. Like Goldsmith's villagers:

> And still they gazed, and still the wonder grew,
> That one small head could carry all he knew.

My last and most moving memory of Dodd is associated with an Easter Sunday evening not long before his death. He was in the nursing-home and I took Communion with him, reading as part of the service the story of the walk to Emmaus. Before we began I said to this Director of the New English Bible, 'I'm going to use the Authorized Version, not the NEB!' He smiled and said, 'I prefer it!' and we chatted about the difference between the liturgical and teaching appositeness of various versions. After the service Dodd said, 'There are two Scripture passages which I now read more often than any others. One we have just read. The other is John 21. For me, these are the most self-authenticating of all testimonies to the resurrection.'

Dodd always acknowledged his debt to his senior at Mansfield, George Buchanan Gray, whose death in 1922 at the age of fifty-seven was a grievous loss to the world of biblical scholarship. A profound and erudite Semitic scholar, Gray was one of the least coherent of lecturers and even in his seminars and tutorials he was far from fluent. Before expressing a judgement on some student's immature conclusion he would produce strange vocal sounds that were his distinctive variants of 'um' and 'ah'. These would reverberate for some time before a more explosive utterance leading to the words 'An interesting point'. Even if subsequently he demolished the student's argument he would not deny this meed of encouragement; in fact, he gave the impression of honestly wishing that he could be proved wrong and the pupil vindicated. With me personally he was wonderfully patient and a great encourager, even convincing me that I was capable of a more advanced Hebrew paper as an extra subject in final Schools. I think of him with lasting affection and as an embodiment of intellectual integrity. As was written of him in a College obituary: 'Truth was the very soul of him.'

J.V. Bartlet, for different reasons, also failed as a lecturer to arrest the attention of his hearers. The main exceptions to this were when during his long and tortuous approach to the end of a sentence we held our breaths and wondered whether, after winding his way through a maze of subordinate clauses, he would reach a logical full stop. He invariably did, even when — as frequently happened — there would be a long pause during which he gazed towards infinity seemingly in search of a clue to the relation of his most recent phrase to the pattern of the whole sentence. Bartles — as we called him — was acutely sensitive to the inattentiveness of the class and was almost morbidly watchful lest any books on which the hearers appeared to be concentrating had nothing to do with the matter in hand. It is credibly reported that one one such occasion he suspended a sentence at a critical point while he interjected the pained reproach, 'I hear the rustle of an alien leaf'. Only once was I rebuked by him. I was offering him my rough translation (very) of Athanasius on the Incarnation. The Greek conjunction *kai* can serve many purposes, to most of which I was regrettably indifferent. In general I found the simple translation 'and' good enough for me. Not so for Bartles. 'My dear Goodall,' he at last broke in, 'I beg you never, never ride roughshod over a *kai*.' In contrast to the obscurity of his style as a lecturer, there were certain occasions when Bartlet prophesied with astonishing lucidity and force. These usually occurred in a discussion group, such as the Nicene Society or the Origen Society. At one of these a member would read a paper on some theological issue; other members would criticize, question, and make their own more or less authoritative contributions to the subject. Meantime his great height (he was well over six feet) would somehow be curled into an easy chair. Then when the timely moment was approaching he would begin to unwind, stand erect, gaze aloft, and utter. Here there was no hesitation, no circumlocution, but a masterly synopsis of the preceding discussion, a swift demolition of faulty arguments and a lucid presentation of his own opinion. He was superb.

My last contact with Bartlet was a touching one. Not long before his death and some years after his retirement I revisited Mansfield to lead a preterminal retreat. After leaving the College I happened to meet Bartlet and we stopped to greet one another. Soon this good man embarked on an elaborate apology for not having come to the College to see me — a wholly unnecessary apology. It led however to a kind of *apologia pro vita sua.* His days were numbered, he said; time was fleeting and there was much he would like still to do. He knew, however, that he could not accomplish it all, and he hoped that some of his former students might take up the work he had left undone. 'For I realize', he said, 'that through my many years as a teacher I have not been as gifted

29

as I could have wished in the art of — how shall I describe it? — I believe the phrase is "getting it across".' I was too moved to speak and he continued, 'I have written a great deal and spoken much but I think I still have something to give. Looking back over the many years in which I have been learning, I think I might now claim with all due modesty that I am almost ripe . . . as a student.' I never saw dear Bartles again but I have not forgotten how much he got across in those moments.

The College combined the work of Chaplain and Tutor in one person and in 1919 we were fortunate that this more junior member of the faculty was Nathaniel Micklem, a charming and uniquely gifted member of a distinguished family. 'Nath', as he was known throughout a vast circle of friends, had made his mark at New College and as a brilliant President of the Oxford Union. A fine classical scholar, a wit of rare vintage and a poet of distinction, he thought theologically with a concern for all things human. In 1919 he published the *Open Light: an enquiry into faith and reality*, following this a year later with *The Galilean: the permanent element in religion*. A group of kindred spirits — Fearon Halliday, Clutton Brock, William Robinson, H.G. Wood, C.H. Dodd, and Nath Micklem — were writing at this time in a manner which spoke effectively to the mood of the nineteen-twenties. Their work reflected the liberal evangelical tradition but it sounded depths not always associated with that debatable term. Micklem left Mansfield in 1921, returning ten years later first as Professor of New Testament and then as Principal. By this time the shadow of Hitler was menacing Europe, and Jewish refugee scholars were seeking asylum in other lands. Oxford, including Mansfield, opened its doors to these and Micklem established close contacts with many of them and with the Confessing Church in Germany. For some years the experience of the German Churches under Hitlerism and National Socialism became a dominating concern in Micklem's thought, and it should not have been surprising, though many found it so, that the emphasis of his theology shifted in the direction of that revival of biblical theology which in turn was greatly influenced by Karl Barth. Micklem was never a typical Barthian, even if such there be, but there were those both in the Free

30

Churches and in Mansfield College itself who failed to see any fundamental correspondence between the Micklem of the *Open Light* and the author of *What is the Faith?*, a challenging and provocative book published in 1936 which restated his theological position and raised fundamental questions about the nature of the Church and its fidelity to the faith. For a time there were consequent misunderstandings which went deep and — as Nath's essay in autobiography later recalled[1] — caused a good deal of personal strain and pain. Happily this period passed and the profound significance of Nath's leadership received the appreciation it deserved.[2]

For a small college — it then numbered only about thirty theological students — a faculty which included Gray, Bartlet, Dodd, and Micklem was a rich endowment. What immediately impressed me as a newcomer was not only the calibre of these men but the lavish manner in which they put their riches of knowledge and friendship at the disposal of the most raw of students. Here was a scholarly *noblesse oblige* which taught me much about the meaning of greatness.

There was another teacher at Mansfield who, in person no less than in office, was the key to the purpose and spirit of the College. This, of course, was the Principal — William Boothby Selbie. About thirty years after I left Mansfield I was visiting Scandinavia in connection with my work with the International Missionary Council and the World Council of Churches. Amongst other responsibilities I had occasion to consult a certain bishop of the Lutheran Church in Denmark. Just before setting out for the appointment I was warned by a young Danish friend that this great and good man was subject to periodical attacks of gout of a particularly virulent character. At such times, said my well-wisher, there was a marked tendency in the episcopal body for nature to withstand grace. He wished for me journeying mercies, especially the mercy of not running into one of the holy man's bad days. I arrived at the town in which I was to meet the bishop; I was welcomed at the station by his wife whose goodwill was

[1] Nathianel Micklem, *The Box and the Puppets.*
[2] I contributed a fuller appraisal and appreciation of Micklem's work to the *Journal* of the United Reformed Church History Society in October 1977 (Vol.I, No.10).

evidently tinged with some anxiety. She immediately began to apologize for the fact that the bishop himself had not come to meet me. 'Unfortunately,' she said, 'this is one of his bad days. He suffers from gout.' As we drove from the station to the house we talked of this and that; then suddenly my hostess said, very wistfully, 'Do you happen to have been at Oxford?' 'Yes,' I answered. 'I suppose you would have been too young to have known one Dr Selbie?' she inquired. 'No', I replied. 'I still think of him as my father-in-God though he has been dead many years.' With an enormous sigh of relief the dear lady said, 'Oh my husband will be pleased! He still idolizes the memory of Dr Selbie.' We reached the Bishop's house. As soon as the door was opened my hostess called out confidently and cheerfully, 'Darling, I've brought someone to see you who knew Dr Selbie.' From that point onwards all was well; I scarcely heard a word about the gout. In most of our conversation we were back in Oxford in the early nineteen-twenties, when, I learned, this Lutheran bishop was reading theology at Christ Church. Ecclesiastically he was in a very different camp from that represented at Mansfield, but early in his stay at Christ Church someone told him that before leaving Oxford he must listen to the best preacher in the University, who could be heard in Mansfield College Chapel. The young Lutheran ordinand went, a little un-believingly; but in the event he was profoundly moved and continued to attend the chapel services for the rest of his time in Oxford. 'It was not only Selbie's preaching which held me,' he said. 'Most of all it was his prayers. They taught me something about the meaning of prayer, especially public prayer, which I have never forgotten.'

This example of what Selbie's ministry meant far beyond the range of the English Free Churches could be multiplied almost indefinitely. Over the years I have found his name to be a passport to friendship in North and South America, in the Middle East and Africa, in India, Ceylon, and the Far East. While this has been due pre-eminently to the character and spirit of the man himself, it also represents a fulfilment of the aims which motivated those who helped to turn Spring Hill College, Birmingham, into Mansfield College, Oxford. The tests which had hitherto prevented Dissenters from entering the University had been removed only in 1870 (the rule preventing non-Anglicans from taking a Divinity degree was only relaxed in 1920 when Selbie was honoured by the award of a DD by special decree). By the time Mansfield was established in 1886, Free Churchmen were entering Oxford in considerable numbers. It was therefore hoped that the College would contribute to the continued nurture in the faith of Free Church graduates in Oxford. At the same time the desire was expressed that as far as possible the College chapel should also provide a ministry to other members of the University, alongside and in co-operation with other preaching and pastoral centres in Oxford. This wider ministry was most powerfully exercised by W.B. Selbie in the years immediately following the first world war. He possessed great pastoral gifts which somehow became known by members of the University of all denominations and none, and in his pulpit ministry he was an astonishing force. He possessed no physical attributes to aid this. He was small in stature, almost insignificant, but from the first word in the opening of an act of worship he spoke with authority. His sermon themes were theologically central — the appeal and challenge of the person of Jesus, the necessity and reality of saving grace, and the demands of a disciplined discipleship, with an emphasis on the disciplined life. He preached without notes though we knew something of the hours of silent prepara-tion, and he used a disconcertingly direct style, not disdaining to use current slang. There was much repetition of familiar phrases but no repetition dimmed their force and no use of slang diminished the dignity and often terror of the Word. But with it all there was an accent of almost heart-breaking caring and pleading and it was this which characterized his prayers. Scripture-reading, sermons, and prayers lifted the worshippers into the presence of the Lord. When Nath Micklem unveiled a portrait of Selbie on a memorable oc-casion he applied to this reserved and yet utterly self-giving servant of the Word the Psalmist's cry 'My heart breaketh for the longing it hath to thy commandments.' I still think of Selbie with an awesome gratitude to my father-in-God, and I do so with an inescapable touch of heart-break as I seem to hear again his voice.

In the first few years after the end of the war the average age of undergraduates in Oxford was considerably higher than would normally have been the case. It is true that youngsters such as Beverley Nichols were making loud noises in the Oxford of the 'twenties, provoking Vera Brittain subsequently to assert that instead of making the world safe for democracy the war had only made Oxford safe for Beverley Nichols, but Oxford in general and Mansfield in particular were now catering very largely for men who had carried great responsibilities during the war years and had known the meaning of danger. At Mansfield the men of my own year had either seen army service or the alternative services offered to conscientious objectors, some of whom had been in prison. A great diversity of backgrounds, experiences, and convictions found a new unity in a common purpose. For me these three years in the College were a unique period of my life and one that I can only think of with a sense of immeasurable indebtedness. I have been privileged to serve on the Governing Body of the College for something more than forty years and I have been blessed by the ministry which a son of mine exercised for eight years as bursar, chaplain, and organist. During a half-century and more I have enjoyed the friendship of five of the College Principals — W.B. Selbie, Nath Micklem, John Marsh, George Caird, and the present incumbent Donald Sykes. This has added to a gratitude which shows no signs of diminishing during a new chapter in which the College, while still concentrating on theological studies, has become a permanent private hall of the University with an enrolment of about ninety students, both graduates and undergraduates, reading in different faculties.

My contemporaries in the College provided a large part of what Mansfield has continued to mean to me. There was Romilly Micklem, a younger brother of Nath, with a less obvious sparkle than his brother but a fastidious scholar and a man of great sensitivity. J.P. Naish, an ardent Quaker who had endured much for his pacifism and had a genius for requiting evil with good, was as scintillating in private conversation as in public debate. He succeeded Buchanan Gray for a few years in the Old Testament Chair though this was not his happiest period. When he left us to become a reader with the Oxford University Press I am not sure whether it was ten or twenty oriental languages which he was able to offer. Lifelong friendships with such fellow-students as

N.A. Turner-Smith, John Whale, C.A. Neeve, and Neville Martin have continued to be my delight and inspiration.

My debt to Mansfield includes all that was made available to me through the friendship of older men whose years in the College much antedated mine. Various circumstances, including the nature of my subsequent work, made this possible, yet from my student days I was encouraged and helped by men whose Oxford years belonged to the era of Fairbairn's principalship. A.E. Garvie welcomed me into his home at New College, London, and discoursed on the necessity for Christian unity. R.F. Horton of Lyndhurst Road, Hampstead, invited me to the first of a series of theological conferences which he launched in 1928 as a Free Church parallel (and corrective!) to H.D.A. Major's Modern Churchmen's movement. I later became secretary and chairman of these Horton conferences and in the meantime one of their greatest gifts to me was their founder's friendship and the inspiration of his mind and spirit. W.J. McAdam of Leeds, Edward Shillito – poet and wit – and that genius in friendship Henry ('Polly') Carter of Cambridge became wonderful friends as well as wise mentors. Towards the end of Carter's long ministry we were chatting about the 'foolishness of preaching' and recalling the most memorable comments made by some of our listeners. Carter declared that the best thing ever said to him after a service came from a seemingly simple old lady: 'Well, Mr Carter,' she said, 'God bless your feeble efforts!' And Henry added, 'The wonderful thing about the ministry is that He does!' When I entered the ministry Carrs Lane Church or 'Meeting House' in Birmingham was renowned for its pulpit tradition. As a boy I sometimes sat under J.H. Jowett, master of elegant speech and a man of great spiritual influence. His successors have all been Mansfield men and my familiar friends, especially Sidney M. Berry whose ready smile and charm aided but only lightly veiled great strength of purpose; Leyton Richards, vocally the most pugilant pacifist I have known, and Leslie Tizard in whom there was a profound depth of spiritual understanding from which he derived the courage to endure the long illness which ended his years on earth at the height of his powers.

To be training for the Christian ministry in 1919 and the early 'twenties was an exhilarating experience. Life was attuned to Rupert Brooke's

> . . . Nobleness walks in our ways again;
> And we have come into our heritage.

It was difficult not to feel — however secretly the assumption
was cherished — that the words of an older writer could be
applied to oneself — 'Who knoweth whether thou art not
come to the Kingdom for such a time as this?' The widespread disillusionment and cynicism of the later 'twenties had
not yet set in. C.E. Montague's essays in disenchantment
came later. It is true that for the more discerning the pre-1914
confidence was gone for ever and many cherished institutions
were being shaken towards their ultimate disappearance.
Nevertheless, there was a reasonable optimism about the outcome of the new era of reconstruction. In the Churches there
was a widespread recognition that radical changes in their life
and worship were needed, yet this was regarded more as an
invigorating opportunity than a daunting problem. Moreover,
contemporary voices were being heard which seemed to
promise a fresh and effective leadership. There was Dick
Sheppard, whose sharpest denunciations had an endearing
quality about them; Tubby Clayton was carrying into peace-
time the Christian camaraderie of Toc H; the passionate and
prophetic notes of Studdert Kennedy were being heard as
forcefully as when he spoke in the role of 'Woodbine Willy'.
William Temple, then a younger voice, was bringing his
combined intellectual and spiritual authority to the Religion
and Life weeks which were commanding great attendance at
the universities. Tissington Tatlow (commonly known as
T-squared) was at the helm of the Student Christian Movement with a group of Free Church associates all well matched
in their considerable gifts of pen and speech — Frank Lenwood, Malcolm Spencer, Hugh Martin, Bill Paton, Robert
Mackie. Not least significant was the powerful pull of the
foreign missionary societies which at that time were evoking
an eager response in money and vocation, relatively un-
troubled by the searching questions which would assail the
confidence of the missionary movement in the years ahead.
Comparable to this zeal for overseas missions — and closely
linked to it in leadership — such an event as COPEC 1926,
the Conference on a Christian Order in Politics, Economics

and Citizenship — seemed to be the beginning of an era in which the implications of the Gospel would be brought more searchingly to bear on the structures of society. Here, it was thought, the Church was finding a new role and fulfilling it with new vigour as part of its mission to go into all the world.

> Bliss was it in that dawn to be alive,
> But to be young was very heaven!

At the heart of this mood there was serious conviction that through the agonies of a world war mankind had learned some lessons from which it would never want to retreat. Co-operation rather than murderous rivalry between nations and communities would be the norm, or at any rate sought-for ideals. Youth would be given its chance in a brave new world. There would be a 'return' to the Christian faith, or at least a new hunger and search for spiritual values and power to express them which would give the Churches their opportunity.

Life did not turn out quite like this. The hedonism of the late 'twenties soon gave place to the ominous sense that all was not well and by the mid-'thirties the 'darkness over Germany' (to recall the title of Amy Buller's tract for the times) began to compel awareness that the sacrifice of millions of lives in one world war had not in itself guaranteed the world against a recurrence, unbelievable as such a prospect seemed to many. Even the clarion if sombre tones of a Karl Barth and the challenging witness of a Confessing Church in Germany spoke only to a limited number of minds and hearts. For the most part the Churches moved into a period of questioning and anxiety, if not of bewilderment. Institutionally, at any rate, they were denied the success in responsiveness which for a time had seemed likely.

Before these clouds descended, however, there was still apparent something of the after-glow of a more prosperous period in the Churches, especially the Free Churches. This institutional prosperity had been bound up with social structures and social habits and the more radical social changes had yet to come or to be felt in their full force. I had already entered upon my ministry before the astonishing moment arrived when, on a home-made 'cat's whisker' receiving set I heard some of the early broadcasts from 2LO.

Prior to this we knew nothing of radio and scarcely imagined the likelihood of television. This vast new world of entertainment and instruction had not yet been created. In the earliest days of my association with church and Sunday school even the cinema was a novelty with most of its potentialities undeveloped. As a child I was taken to the Curzon Hall, Birmingham, to see some early 'moving pictures' which gave promise of replacing and improving on the 'panorama' which we went to see at Christmas time in the same hall. In this period, for large numbers of people the church was their entertainment and cultural centre, whether or not it was also their household of faith. Not many years before I was born the term 'Aston Villa' described only an amateur football club created for young men associated with the Aston Villa Wesleyan Methodist Church where I was baptized. Professional sport on the scale it has now assumed was a long way ahead. The churches were the home of literary societies, choral societies, amateur orchestras, dramatic societies, and games clubs. One of the best stocked libraries from which I borrowed as a child was the Sunday school library. My first savings went into a penny bank run by the church. Sunday school anniversaries were annual musical festivals in which choirs of several hundred voices 'rendered' programmes which had been rehearsed in weekly sessions for some months. It was within the context of this recreational and 'improving' social service that the 'princes of the pulpit' added their distinctive contribution. Some of these drew a large following because of their known eccentricities. I was entranced as a child by a famous ornament of Methodism, Mark Guy Pearse, whose sermons were interspersed with selections from an extensive repertoire of delightful Cornish stories delivered with the skill of a professional entertainer. This good man could generally be relied upon to get so worked up during his utterances that he would stride to and fro in the vast pulpit, weep aloud on occasion, clamber up and down the long flight of pulpit steps while still talking, or threaten to go home because he could see that his congregation of hell-deserving sinners had become Gospel hardened. It was great fun. I recall also a Congregational minister (for whom I later developed a great respect) whose church became filled to capacity largely because it was reported that he had worn a yellow waistcoat on Sunday and said 'Damn' in the pulpit and addressed the children of his congregation as 'little devils' (probably not without reason). Eccentricities apart, sermon-tasting had a recognized place amongst the godly. The form of discourse, the relevance of the illustrations, the manner of its delivery and whether it was preaching for a verdict or too insubstantial in doctrine and manner 'to save the soul of a titmouse' were matters for serious consideration and discussion, and the discussion was part of the simple diet of a well-spent Sunday. For many Free Church families even the choice of a holiday resort was considerably influenced by what was known about the stronger churches in the town. Should we go to Bournemouth again to hear J.D. Jones at Richmond Hill? Have you heard Rhondda Williams at Union Church, Brighton? Or when in Brighton should you sit under that renegade Congregationalist H.J. Campbell, whose dulcet tones could now be beard from an Anglican pulpit? No good Free Church business-man if in Birmingham for a weekend would miss a visit to Carrs Lane Meeting House to hear J.H. Jowett or Sidney Berry, and a visit to Manchester would surely include a service at Bowden Downs Congregational Church where one of Alexander Mackennal's successors would be holding forth in the great tradition.

Although the theological content of sermons, whether explicit or implicit, varies greatly with preachers, much of the best preaching of the 'twenties came from men who were greatly influenced by such scholars as John Oman, William Temple, C.H. Dodd, B.H. Streeter, teachers and writers who for all their differences stood for a faith rooted in the classical centralities but given contemporary relevance by exegetical, philosophical, and psychological insights and skills. While P.T. Forsyth had yet to be accorded a belated honour in his own country, there were at least a few preachers sounding Forsythian notes as a kind of prelude to later Barthian preaching. Again, though this also applied to a somewhat eclectic circle, the penetrating mind, voice, and wit of Bernard Manning were compelling a profounder understanding of the meaning of worship and preaching. All in all it was not at a superficial or trivial level, nor was it with complacency, that the Church and its ministers were facing the new demands and needs of a post-war generation.

My own ministry began in 1922 when I was ordained at Trinity Congregational Church, Walthamstow. Six years later I left Walthamstow for New Barnet where I ministered for eight years in another Congregational church. This was only a stone's throw from St Augustine's Presbyterian Church where H.H. Farmer was minister, one of the choicest spirits in the Christian ministry — philosopher, theologian and friend. We worked closely together and the two churches eventually became one some years before Congregationalism and Presbyterianism found a common expression in the United Reformed Church. I was fortunate in the two congregations I served. It is generally recognized that a young minister's first charge can either make or break him, or — if break is too strong a term — he can suffer serious shocks in the transition from the vision and hopes of his period of training to the realities of the local situation. No beginner could have been placed in a better nurturing ground than Walthamstow provided for me. The congregation was never large but the fellowship was strong and far from inward-looking. The world mission of the Church was a reality; we had strong links with the London Missionary Society and on one wall of the church there was a notice indicating that the church was affiliated to the World Alliance for Promoting International Friendship through the Churches. This was one of the earlier organizations which contributed to the eventual formation of the World Council of Churches. It had begun to take shape in the years immediately preceding 1914 and sought to develop Christian relationships across national frontiers in the cause of peace. In local social, educational, and public service many of the members of Trinity were deeply involved, and in relation to the size of the congregation the proportion of young people was high. There was certainly no lack of challenge, opportunity, or encouragement for a young minister. This was no less true of my second pastoral charge at New Barnet, in spite of differences between the two localities and the fact that my years in Barnet included some sharper testings.

I began my ministry in fear and trembling and there is a sense in which I have never lost these feelings during the fifty-seven years that have passed since my ordination. This applies especially to the two aspects of ministering which have always meant most to me — the conduct of worship and the pastoral ministry or 'cure of souls', to use an archaic but searching term. The conduct of worship, including preaching, has seldom been other than a deeply satisfying experience. Yet the preparation — of material and of myself — has always been a travail and often an exhausting struggle. The fears associated with it continue to provide the main ingredients of occasional nightmares of the anxiety type. Yet in the event, when once a service of worship has begun I have no tremors, only a sense of assurance which is quite different from self-confidence. As regards the pastoral work, I am fond of people and enjoy making contacts and enlarging my knowledge of our human diversities, glorious or terrible. No interior happiness is greater than the realization that through speaking, listening (especially) and both, a natural caring for people in need has been used in some measure by the grace that heals, comforts, guides, and empowers. But I have never ceased to fear lest the wrong or inadequate word or the wrong timing of a question or comment or fear of silence should prove a hindrance to that 'cure' which I believe to proceed from the divine caring of which I am a minister.

I had no wish to leave New Barnet or to end my service as what is sometimes called 'a working minister', one engaged in a local pastorate. I moved to other work simply because the summons to it seemed imperative. In my subsequent ministry I have never lacked opportunities for the conduct of worship or pastoral service but these have not been quite the same as those related to a local community in which there are deep continuities despite the comings and goings of a mobile era. Certainly I have never lost my conviction that the local church is the place where the Church universal lives or dies. There can therefore be no place where the role of the ministry is more important or more personally satisfying.

4 INTO ALL THE WORLD

In 1922, my last year at Oxford, my wife and I made an offer of life-time service to the London Missionary Society.[1] Doris, my wife, was a medical doctor and we hoped that there might be some way in which her professional skills could be useful in a dual appointment. The Society decided, however, that it could not send us overseas. The decision was chiefly due to an unsatisfactory medical report but there was the further difficulty that under the rules of the Mission a wife could not hold an appointment independent of her husband's. So Doris continued in general practice, later combining with this a large amount of voluntary work with the Girl Guide movement, especially in the movement's 'extension' service with handicapped girls. She has always brought a touch of genius to such service and in this, as in all her professional work, she has responded to a great vocation with an unsparing dedication.

Our commitment to the cause of overseas missions continued, of course, despite lack of opportunity to serve abroad. Early in my ministry I was appointed to the Board of the London Missionary Society and remained a member or officer of it for the best part of half a century.[2]

I was also closely associated with the missionary training colleges in Selly Oak, Birmingham, and at one stage I reluctantly declined an invitation to become 'Professor of Missions' in the colleges. After my retirement from the World Council of Churches I was delighted to fulfil this role for a few terms and to become much involved in the rapidly developing work of the Federation of the Selly Oak Colleges, under the stimulating leadership and friendship of its President, Paul Clifford. This happy association only ended officially in 1977 when I felt it was time to relinquish my

[1] Now known as the Council for World Mission.
[2] I was commissioned to write the third volume of the Society's history in commemoration of its Triple Jubilee (*The History of the London Missionary Society, 1895–1945*, Oxford University Press, 1965).

membership and vice-chairmanship of the Federation's Council.

In 1936 I was invited to join the staff of the London Missionary Society with secretarial responsibility for the work in India and the South Pacific. The Society took a justifiable pride in its roll of honour. Founded towards the end of the eighteenth century it sent John Williams to the South Seas, Wilhelm Ringeltaube to India, Robert Morrison to China, Johannes Vanderkemp, David Livingstone, and Robert Moffat to Africa, David Jones to Madagascar, John Smith to the West Indies, James Chalmers and William Lawes to Papua. The great succession was nobly maintained by scores of men and women who, whether well-publicized or little-known, served with valour and great devotion, many of them giving a lifetime's service to the land of their adoption.

There have always been critics of the missionary enterprise and there have never lacked people ready and eager to accept caricature for fact in their understanding of the word 'missionary'. Today the term is again under a cloud and even in large parts of the Church universal there is questioning and uncertainty about the place of the foreign missionary movement in today's world. For my own part, throughout my Christian education and experience there has been an inescapable compulsion to let all the world know the good news of the Christian revelation. As I shall try to say more fully in a later chapter, I firmly believe that in Jesus Christ there is a unique disclosure of the nature of God, his relation to man, and his dealings with us. This disclosure carries with it light upon the meaning of our existence. It tells us what life is all about, what it means to live life to the full, and where we can find the power to do so. Other religions are concerned with these things and I cannot deny that the Spirit which we know in its fullness through Jesus Christ has been at work in all ages and in response to all the deepest yearnings of humanity. It is part of the Christian missionary obligation to understand the other religions, to learn from them, and receive correction from them. But this does not diminish the responsibility for sharing with their adherents all that we believe about Jesus Christ and all that we are experiencing of his grace and truth. The much used word 'dialogue' in its application to discourse between the adherents of different religions calls for a greater humility and openness on the part of Christians than has sometimes been apparent in the past. No one would now thunder against other faiths in such terms as were used in 1898, when, with furious zeal, a preacher declared: 'Ethnic religions smell of the charnel house. Hinduism is stupefaction. Mohammedanism is putrefaction. Buddhism is obliteration.'[3] This was not exactly the wooing note which lecturers in homiletics used to urge upon their students. It is a sign of progress in Christian understanding and in our apprehension of grace that we now recoil from such an approach to evangelism. Nevertheless, though the Christian is a humble learner of all God's ways, there can be no muting of the conviction that we have seen in Christ the way, the truth, and the life, and that ultimately there is 'no other name' of comparable significance. A close friend from whom I have learned much in this field of thought and obedience was the late Hendrik Kraemer of Holland,[4] who taught and exemplified the view that the Christian approach to other faiths must be compounded of 'radical humility and downright intrepidity' — utter humility before the testimony of other believers, yet unswerving fidelity to what we believe to be the truth as it is in Jesus.

The invitation to become a secretary of the LMS reached me a few hours before I was due to leave for South Africa. A generous-minded friend, thinking I was in need of a holiday, had made it possible for me to go with my eldest son, then a boy of thirteen, on a voyage to Cape Town, with time for a few weeks inland travel. This had seemed a good opportunity to visit some missionary friends, and it turned out that I wrote my letter of acceptance to the Society from the home of an older Mansfield man at a place called Tiger Kloof. This was a famous educational institution (since closed under changes in the educational policy of South Africa) whose principal was A.J. Haile, one of the wisest and most lovable of men. All that I saw during my few days at Tiger Kloof made the Society's invitation irresistible, and my gratitude for the new opportunity was heightened as we continued our journey into what was then the Bechuanaland Protectorate

---

[3] George Lorrimer in *Missionary Sermons* (Carey Press, undated but the sermons were preached in the '80s and '90s).
[4] See further pp. 85, 89, 95.

with its capital in Serowe. This was the home of the Bamangwato people whose former ruler, King Khama, has become a legendary figure in missionary history. King or Chief Khama had been the central figure in a great mass movement to Christianity. Under his influence and with the help of LMS missionaries the Church of the Bamangwato people became the most cherished institution in their community. It was equipped with strong African leadership and although the missionaries played an important and welcome role they were no more than partners with their African colleagues. I met the widow of Chief Khama, Queen Semane, a stately lady of undoubted authority, and my son and I were warmly welcomed and entertained by the Regent, Chief Tshekedi, uncle of the present head of the Botswana State, Sir Seretse Khama. In these later years I have enjoyed a particularly warm friendship with a former student of Tiger Kloof — one of many such who have achieved distinction in public affairs. This is Miss Garsitwe Chiepe, at the time of writing Minister of Commerce and Industry in the Botswana Government. She is a graduate and honorary LL.D. of Bristol University and was for some years Botswana High Commissioner in London. She combined this post with that of Ambassador to several European countries and Botswana's representative on the European Economic Community. This very dear friend is a gracious and accomplished witness to the benefits of a Christian education as well as to the gifts and characteristics of her people.

It was necessary that having accepted the proffered secretaryship I should as soon as possible visit the areas of work for which I was responsible. These were India and the South Pacific. It was reported that early in the history of the LMS one of my predecessors had sent a telegram to a pioneer missionary containing only the words 'Possess India'. This was a somewhat tall order even allowing for the worthiest Christian zeal. Soon after I landed in India I put one of the obvious questions of a newcomer to a senior missionary. In answer to my question he said, 'If you'd asked me years ago when I had been in the country only a few months I would have given you a complete and confident reply. Having been here for over thirty years I don't know what to say.' I have never forgotten the significance of this reply, especially when my questioners have clearly expected some illuminating generalization. For example, I was aware that I could know nothing about India until I had seen her countless villages. During my seven-months tour I spent some time in about a hundred and forty of these, itinerating with missionaries, camping in place after place and travelling on foot, by bullock-cart, or doubtful car along doubtful roads within a circuit of villages. I sometimes slept in a tent, sometimes on an uncertain bed in a travellers' bungalow, having first looked for the inventory item 'Chairs, bug-proof, 1', or — most welcomely — in a missionary's home. On one of these itinerating days I think I reached my record in peripatetic activity. I laid two foundation stones, opened a new football field by kicking off, and gave eight addresses. At the end of my tour I calculated that, if I had tried to cover all the villages of India at my rate of progress through a hundred-and-forty of them, it would have taken me about two hundred years to see all the villages which statistics told me made up the whole. What is village India like? And what of urban India which, even when I first saw a little of it forty years ago, included some of the greatest industrial enterprises in the world? What is India like? In my subsequent addresses on India, I used to begin with the innocent understatement, 'India is a large place'.

The main work of the LMS in India was in the south, in four language areas, Tamil, Telugu, Kanarese, and Malayalam. On a smaller scale there was work, principally educational and medical, in and around Calcutta and in the Murshidabad area. I began my work a decade before political independence and there was a marked distinction between the provinces of British India and the India of the Princes or Native States with which Britain held special treaty relationships. The Madras Province and the States of Mysore and Travancore constituted the chief areas of the Society's work. In the larger towns there was educational and medical work as well as evangelistic activity, but it was the rural areas which claimed most attention at the time of which I am writing. Here the Christian population was drawn predominantly from the lower castes and those who at different periods were called outcastes, untouchables, harijans, or somewhat euphemistically the scheduled castes. The majority of these owed their Christian faith to mass movements, that is the embracing of

46

Christianity by a whole community under the influence of leaders who had themselves first become converts. It is worth recalling that large parts of Europe, including Britain, originally become Christian by a similar sociological process. Although the poverty of villagers in South India was far less horrifying than what I later saw in the appalling squalor and degradation of such a place as Calcutta, I experienced in full the shock of inexperience in seeing, feeling, and smelling the level of existence endured by the thousands of families amongst whom I moved during these months, and I may recall what I have indicated in an earlier chapter that my own family had lived not very far above the poverty line and that I was by no means unfamiliar with life in the slums of Birmingham. Towards the end of one long day's touring among the villages, at nightfall driving back to a missionary's home, we had given a lift to a young Indian Christian teacher. We stopped at the outskirts of the village where he lived and left him to walk to his home. Having said a 'Good-bye and God bless you', he called out as he disappeared into the darkness, 'Don't forget us.' How could I?

The village teachers were generally also village pastors. Forty years ago the main, and often the only possibility of primary education for such communities as I was visiting was through the work of the missions. Many of the teacher-pastors had themselves received only an exceedingly elementary education, though the need for more adequate teacher training and provision for higher education was a high priority in mission policy. In the larger centres I saw something of the enormous contribution being made under Christian auspices at schools and colleges of various grades leading up to universities of world-wide fame such as the Madras Christian colleges for men and women. Medical work similarly covered a great range from elementary hygiene and first aid to the advanced surgery of a network of well-equipped hospitals and the highly sophisticated medical schools of Vellore in the south and Ludhiana in the north.

This first visit of mine to India, and many later tours in numerous countries, have left me with a lasting regret that in spite of having spent several decades in the whole-time service of the missionary enterprise I have not been privileged to serve abroad except 'on tour'. I have learned much about the meaning of missionary service, its hazards, its frustrations, disillusionments, and failures, as well as its glories and triumphs. Missionaries of various nationalities and denominations have opened their homes and hearts to me — Indians, Africans, West Indians, Pacific Islanders, Chinese, and Japanese have been my friends and counsellors, leaders and partners. But even when my tours have been lengthy and their circumstances most revealing I have remained aware that I could not know 'under the skin' all that it means to transfer one's life to another culture, to substitute for my mother tongue another speech, to acquire a fundamentally different way of thinking and feeling, with all the enormous gains as well as demands which such a translation of life entails. Reflecting on this, I find myself wondering greatly today what is in fact happening to the personalities of the thousands of immigrants now making their homes in these western lands and in Britain in particular. Is their experience an enriching process or . . . ? I have met misfits amongst the missionaries, some mistaken in their vocation, some not capable of the strain, or sufficiently open in spirit to grapple with new experiences and testings, but by far the greater number of those I have known have made me envious as well as appreciative of what they have allowed life and their special vocation to make of them.

The first mission hospital which I visited in India happened to be one of the most famous — the South Travancore Medical Mission at Neyyoor. Medical work had been started here by the LMS in 1828 and eventually the hospital was reputed to be the largest medical mission hospital in the world in terms of the number of patients treated annually. Its distinction at the time of my visit was largely due to the character and skill of the missionary in charge, Dr T.H. Somervell — Everest climber, painter and musician, and a surgeon of great eminence. I had known Somervell's father in England where he was Honorary Treasurer of the LMS. The family's enthusiasm for Christian missions prompted Howard while in India to visit Neyyoor. He did this immediately after taking part in the 1921 Everest expedition in which his friends Mallory and Irvine were killed. Writing later of the effect which this visit to Neyyoor had on him, he said: 'I saw the thing which changed the entire plan of my life, something far more impressive than the mighty Himalayas, far more compelling than the call of the mountains. That something was the unrelieved suffering of India.'[5] The rest of his life was dominated by awareness of this need, seen in the light of his deep Christian faith and the discipleship to which he was committed. I recall walking with 'T.H.S.' some miles from Neyyoor when an Indian ran up to him, pulled out his shirt and disclosed a post-operational scar. 'Look!' cried the Indian gleefully, 'You did this.' The two then chipped one another like a couple of schoolboys. On another occasion I saw an outcaste run to Howard, fall at his feet and 'take the dust'. Howard's response was immediately to drop to the ground and return the gesture. 'That's the only way I can deal with that sort of thing,' said Howard to me. When he died in 1975 at the age of 83, the news of his going was cabled to Neyyoor. Within a few hours Indian friends secured an enlarged photograph of him which they carried as a banner around the town in a procession of remembrance and thanksgiving. This was seventeen years after he had left Neyyoor and at a time when the role of the missionary in the eyes of the Indians had radically changed. Eventually a commemorative plaque was placed in the Neyyoor Church. It reads:

In Grateful Remembrance

of Dr T.H. SOMERVELL, MA, MB, B.Ch. FRCS, OBE

Who proclaimed the Gospel through his
LIFE and KNIFE
In Neyyoor from 1923 to 1948

WORLD KNOWN MOUNTAINEER!
A SURGICAL WIZARD!
AN UNASSUMING ARTIST!
AND ABOVE ALL A GOOD SAMARITAN!

Born 16.4.1890 — Died 23.1.75.

'Only remembered by what we have done.'

Erected by the Neyyoor Congregation and
Dedicated 23.1.76.

[5] T.H. Somervell, *After Everest* (Hodder and Stoughton, 1936).

After his death Mrs Somervell found amongst his papers a letter from a Hindu written to Howard many years previously. Its closing salutation read:

Yours in the name of J. Christ Esq. whom you so closely resemble.

Howard Somervell's gifts and achievements inevitably resulted in worldwide fame though this was something which he never sought and always treated with his characteristic humour and a kindly disdain. Innumerable other missionaries, equally unsparing of themselves, fulfilled the same vocation in places and circumstances which commanded no public attention and I should be rendering a grave disservice to T.H.S. without using his story mainly as a tribute to the scores of missionaries whose commitment to a great vocation has been every bit as complete and fruitful. Amongst these many, I recall the wise and accomplished Hilda Pollard, Medical Superintendent of the mission hospital at Erode in the Madras Presidency. Lovely to look upon to the end of her days, with dignity and grace in her bearing, she worked for years in primitive surroundings, trusted and loved by the poorest of the poor who found their way to the hospital from villages many miles distant. There was then no electricity in the hospital. Dr Pollard and her young colleagues, another doctor and a nursing superintendent, would perform operations by the light of a primus lamp in a hospital which had no running water or flush toilets, and was set in a town which still had open drains. Another engaging medical missionary was Cecil Cutting, the superintendent of a hospital at Chikballapur in the Mysore State. Cecil seemed to have been born with a bedside manner. He was gifted with an instinctive sympathy and a most reassurring presence. I could never understand how he got through all his demanding professional and administrative work, for he gave everybody the feeling that time did not matter. Callers could take as long as they wanted over the telling of their complaints and troubles, with further leisure thrown in just for gossip. Cutting never missed a natural opportunity to talk about that friend who had time for everybody — Jesus Christ — but if the conversation went in this direction it was as free from pietism as any of the fascinating tales he could bring out of his extensive repertoire. He was, and still is, a marvellous raconteur with a keen eye and ear for the bizarre and embarrassing incident, especially when it could be embellished with a few gruesome medical details. I remember sauntering through Chikballapur with him and wondering if I should ever get back to a meal or he to his hospital work. All the town knew him. He would stop to return a greeting, then squat down and begin gossiping in Kanarese. He would then be joined by others and soon there would be a circle of Indians listening, laughing, wagging their heads, seemingly with all eternity at their disposal.

This chapter is about more than the missionaries and I must leave room for other things, but I cannot fail to record my profoundest salute to the memory of the senior missionary who more than any other guided my steps through the years of my LMS secretaryship. This was George Parker who, at the time when our friendship began, held a position of general oversight of the Society's work in India, and was a wonderful *pastor pastorum* to young and old. I have known few men as wise as he in dealing with his fellows and proving a very present help in time of trouble. Parker had served for many years in both North and South India and after his retirement he responded to an urgent need for help in training African pastors at Tiger Kloof. He was widely read and maintained a high standard of scholarship amidst the least congenial conditions. We enjoyed frequent correspondence through the years, and I loved him dearly. Amongst the experiences which have left the everlasting Why unanswered for me, except in faith, is the memory of my last visit to him in England at the end of his days. He looked and sounded his dear self, sprucely dressed and as gracious as ever in bearing, but except for one fleeting moment he could give no sign of recollecting any of his earlier years. The decades of his lavish service in India and Africa had apparently been blotted out of a mind which no longer possessed the power of recall. *Sunt lacrimae rerum. . .*

Although I saw vestiges of what is sometimes referred to as the period of the patriarchal missionaries, even forty years ago this role was fast disappearing. Indian leadership had long been in welcome evidence and the missionaries were working in partnership with, and sometimes subordinate to their

Indian colleagues in educational institutions and in the care of those indigenous churches which are now known as the Church of South India and the Church of Northern India.[6]

Beyond my work with missionaries and Indian churchmen I took as many opportunities as possible to meet Indians in other areas of responsibility. In Madras I discussed educational policy with the influential Rajagopalachari (of whom more later). In Trivandrum I was given a private audience by the Maharajah of Travancore, a charming and somewhat diffident youth who was reputed to be dependent for his authority on his powerful mother, the Maharani. Here also I met the formidable C.P. Ramaswamy Ayar, the Dewan or Prime Minister of Travancore — a fascinating talker, suave but determined, a controversialist whom a former British Secretary of State for India credited with possessing the most acute mind of any Indian with whom he had had dealings. In a public greeting to me C.P. enlarged on 'those two catholic religions, Hinduism and Christianity, which should regard one another as colleagues in a common enterprise.' With all his courtesy and often generous co-operation with the missions, he left me in no doubt that from his point of view Hinduism would remain the most influential partner in the 'common enterprise'.

A slightly unusual encounter gave me a glimpse of what could happen in some parts of the India of the Princes. This was in a tiny state called Banganapalle, best known, I was told, for the quality of its mangoes. After visiting a number of village schools and churches in the State I arrived at the capital, where I was to be the guest of the Dewan for the night. It was dark when I arrived and I was met at the out-skirts of the village by a procession of flaming torches and escorted to the State guest house to the sound of martial music. The sovereign of the State, or Nawab, was on a pilgrimage to Mecca so in his absence the Dewan looked after me. He had only recently come down from Oxford and was reputed to be the youngest Dewan in India. He was invested with sovereign rights on the departure of his superior but

[6] I have written in greater detail about the emergence of these churches and the changes in missionary policy which their coming into existence has demanded, in my *History of the London Missionary Society, 1895-1945.*

unfortunately there was no money left in the State treasury with which also to invest him. Banganapalle covered less than 300 square miles. It had a population of 40,000 housed in sixty villages, and the annual revenue of the government was about £18,000. Nevertheless, this parochial administration was being conducted in the lordly language of sovereignty and some of the methods of the Middle Ages. I had a delightful evening with the young Dewan whose conversation was pretty and lively. What plays had I seen lately? Did I know that passion fruit cocktail which they serve at the Dorchester? Had I been to St Moritz recently? Would I like a gift of land for a church? Did I consider that the Group Movement placed too much emphasis on public confession? Early next morning I was awakened by the sound of bugles summoning the State forces to parade. I tumbled out to look at them but they numbered only half a dozen policemen, whose sergeant was doing his best to thunder at the troops in the manner of the Brigade of Guards.

Some years before I went to India I had met Gandhi in London when he was attending one of the abortive Round Table conferences on independence. It was good to renew his acquaintance in Calcutta, where he was living for a time in 1937. My appointment with him coincided with one of his silent periods so I was led to the roof-top where he was resting and told that I might share his silence with him. So I squatted near him and some time later I could have said, as Mark Twain once remarked to an uncommunicative dinner partner, 'We have enjoyed a most interesting silence together'. After a time Gandhi stood up and began to walk to and fro. Still without speaking he gestured to me to take his arm and walk with him. I was glad when eventually he sat down again, bidding me do the same. He then said, 'Now let us talk'. Like most of his visitors, I was impressed by the vigour and sense of power residing in that frail figure. Though disdaining all the trappings of sophistication he could meet and outwit politicians and the wielders of temporal authority. He possessed a formidable will and used great subtlety in accomplishing his ends. In our brief conversation about the most important things of life he paid his familiar testimony to the influence of Jesus and reiterated what he had often said and written: 'If India is to discover for itself the living essence of Christianity missionaries must either leave India or radically alter their methods and cease to proselytize.' I doubt if I succeeeded in convincing him that we saw a fundamental difference between evangelism and proselytization.

Another great Indian politician who impressed me at this time with his obvious ability, not least in diplomatic conversation, was the then President of the Congress Party, Subhas Chandra Bose. He entertained me at tea with witty conversation and with the ease of a man of the world. He was an enigmatic figure, reputedly involved in Bengal terrorism, and later associated with a proscribed Indian 'National Army'. He disappeared during the war after joining forces with the Japanese. I recall his genial manner and especially one of his more serious moments when he said, 'Christian thought has come to stay in India. The Bible in any case will always be with us. I have often found myself using its language when I have felt most deeply. Nevertheless, Christianity has been spoilt for us by its association with the British Raj.'

Bengal provided a welcome opportunity for me to visit Santineketan, the home of Rabindranath Tagore, and of his University or Centre of International Culture. The library with its treasures and the renowned art school greatly impressed me but I felt I had to revise my assumptions about universities as places of academic discipline. 'Why work?', said one of the students to a tutor who told me of the incident. 'Isn't this Santineketan, the Abode of Peace?' My main purpose, of course, was if possible to meet Tagore and I was rewarded by a long talk with him. He conversed with ease and with a pleasant humour . . . and looked so beautiful in his calm dignity that I could soon have become bemused into feeling that if he had only passed the time of day I should have regarded the observation as a gem of pure wisdom. He made what seemed to me a surprising comment on one of the matters on the agenda of my official responsibilities during the tour. Around the years 1936 and 1937 the widespread agitation for removing the disabilities of the depressed classes inevitably touched the Christian missions for it was towards the uplift of these classes that some of their most significant work had been directed. Gandhi's ceaseless efforts on their behalf were becoming effective in many ways including the opening of the Hindu temples to them. Amidst the political ferment surrounding this issue there were rumours of a possible mass movement on a mammoth scale from these classes into the Christian Church, largely for social and political reasons. In Bombay I had met one of the foremost political agitators for reform, Dr Bhimrao Ranji Ambedkar, a graduate of the London School of Economics and a member of the English Bar, who was now a leading member of the Bombay Legislative Assembly. At the time of my visit there was much talk about the possibility that, through his powerful leadership, Ambedkar might swing millions of his followers into the Christian Church. The missions naturally had mixed feelings about this prospect despite their long record of service to these classes and their respect for Ambedkar as one of the most powerful fighters for human rights. I asked Ambedkar about these rumours and he replied that he was seriously considering initiating the kind of movement of which I had heard, 'But', he added, 'which Church? You are so denominationally divided that if I told my followers to embrace Christianity I shouldn't know where to go or to take them. Hadn't you better put your Christian house in order?' The rebuke was irrefutable. I talked with Tagore about all this and he said emphatically that he hoped the depressed classes would find their freedom in Christianity. Hinduism, he said, would gradually open its doors more widely to them but its concessions would prove very limited compared with all that Christianity could offer. Within a short time after this it became clear that no such mass movement was projected or likely, not least because of the adoption of more generous social policies by political leaders. But the observations of both Ambedkar and Tagore were for me of more than passing significance. Does the Church universal in its mission to the world give convincing evidence of a power to unite mankind in that service which is perfect freedom? Years later than these encounters with two dissimilar but very great men I heard that not long before his death in 1956 Ambedkar had embraced the Buddhist faith. The news prompted some searching reflections.

About ten years after this first visit to India I re-visited the country during the last stages of the stormy progress towards independence. Britain was then in process of handing over final authority not to one India but to a partitioned continent which had resulted in the creation of a separate Pakistan. The appalling conflicts between Muslims and Hindus were abating but the two-way trek of refugees — Muslims from India and Hindus from Pakistan — with its accompanying misery was heart-breakingly in evidence. I was consulting with the National Christian Council of India about the relief operations in which the Christian agencies were co-operating with government and other relief agencies, and I spent an unforgettable few days visiting the refugee camps which had been hastily improvised when the storm broke. I recall a day when, in company with a missionary of the Church Missionary Society, Dr Harry Holland, I drove for about twenty miles alongside a weary procession of the homeless as they moved in search of rest and security. Hour after hour I stood with Holland and his fellow-workers on an army lorry which was moving slowly up the Grand Trunk Road from Delhi to the north-west. The road was dead straight and I looked along the miles of it until it dipped over the horizon and as far as I could see the pitiful procession of the dispossessed was shuffling towards the edge of the world with their burdens. Every now and then our lorry stopped and Dr Holland jumped down to give some first aid treatment to those who had fallen in their tracks. For most of them it was last aid and they died where they dropped. We arrived at a transit camp a few hours after another procession of 70,000 had stopped there. Two thousand of these had already become victims of cholera and eight hundred of them were soon dead. We could smell the camp miles before we got there. I visited another camp at a place called Hamuyan's Tomb where on that day I was told about 26,000 Muslims were awaiting their next move. I am not sure whether it was more ironical or appropriate that so many victims of fear should be encamped amongst the sepulchral glories of the past. I was shown round by the camp commandant, a young Indian army officer, whose attention was divided between ensuring that I should not miss a choice bit of mosaic in which the memory of an emperor's barber was enshrined and that I should take notice of the efforts being made to deal with the spread of infection in the camp.

With such impressions as these painfully upon my mind and heart I went to New Delhi for further discussions with some of the Government officials. The Viceroy, Lord Mount-batten, was in London negotiating the final stages of the transfer of power. In his absence I was received by the Acting-Viceroy Rajagopalacharya, familiarly known as Rajaji. I had met him ten years previously in Madras, where I was impressed by the mutual respect, strong enough to survive acute differences of opinion and policy, which clearly prevailed between this powerful Hindu politician, later to be Govenor-General of an independent India, and the Christian missionaries. It was a strange experience to be escorted by British officers through the corridors of departing power, into the Viceroy's room in the Viceregal Lodge. There I was greeted by this impressive Indian whose natural *gravitas* was deepened by the events in which he was playing such a historic part. We talked for twenty minutes or so about relief work and the role of the Christian Council of India in it and I then rose to leave. 'Don't go yet,' said Rajaji. 'Sit down and tell me about my old friends and enemies, the missionaries.' So we chatted about some of the LMS folk who had often crossed swords with him in Madras on educational and other policies. We gossiped for some time in relaxed fashion and again I got up to leave. Rajaji remained sitting, looking out of the window and resting his chin on his hand. There was a long silence and at length he said, 'I have to confess that those days were better than these. At least we knew who were our friends and who our enemies. But now . . . who knows?'

I was greatly moved. It did not and could not occur to me that this valiant fighter for independence was lauding the days of the British Raj at the expense of his own people. I could not think of it as a confession of failure or loss of belief in the cause to which he had given himself. In his voice and face and in the dignity and courtesy with which he said good-bye I could see only greatness − a greatness aware of the costliness of achievement and humbled by a sense of the awful responsibility of power and the precariousness of all human ambitions and accomplishments. In that moment Rajaji embodied for me not only the hopes and fears of India but the fears, hopes, and needs of all humanity.

I did not visit my second main sphere of secretarial responsibility − the Pacific Islands − until 1939, an ominous year.

I set sail for a round-the-world journey on the day that Hitler marched into Prague and shattered Neville Chamberlain's hope of peace in our time. My voyage had been planned some months before and I was booked to travel on the German liner *Europa*. By a grim coincidence the first day's menu included the item Prague Ham.

During the next fourteen months my task took me to Samoa, the Cook Islands and Niue, the Gilbert and Ellice Islands, Ocean Island and Nauru, and Papua. I travelled on almost every kind of vessel — frail dug-out canoes, Samoan long boats as skilfully constructed as Oxford or Cambridge eights but three times as long, river launches, sea-going launches, cargo boats, and trading vessels, and for about four months my home was on a 200-ton auxiliary schooner owned by the London Missionary Society and named after the pioneer missionary John Williams. My boat was the fifth in a line of ships similarly named until the succession ended in 1971 with the sale of the *John Williams VII*. The fifth in the line could touch a maximum of seven knots under full sail with her auxiliary engines at full power, though we covered long distances at no more than two or three knots. The ship was capable of every kind of motion and I sometimes had the impression that her aquabatics included the art of turning turtle and doing everything except sink. There were moments when I almost wished she could do this. To ease the anguish which I suffered in my tiny cabin I slept on deck as often as I could. As the deck was frequently laden with tens of thousands of coconuts (the currency by which school fees were paid) my mattress would be sandwiched between great blocks of these, lashed together for safety and adding their aroma to that of engine oil, cooking smells from the galley, and other varieties. I used to recall a diary entry of one of those eighteenth-century parsons who, in recounting an uncomfortable voyage, boasted that in the whole course of it he was only ill once but the malady lasted from embarkation to disembarkation. Whatever I felt at the time I am glad to have experienced all that my voyage on the *John Williams* entailed, and I cherish a grateful memory of the captain, the most mildly mannered little man who ever went to sea, and who surprisingly bore the name of Captain Kettle. He was a good seaman, quietly devoted to the work of the Society.

The terms South Seas and Pacific Islands still retain something of their glamour and romantic appeal, fostered by the needs of tourism, whatever gulf now exists between advertisements and wares. I saw many disillusioning factors but there was much more that equalled and even exceeded imagined loveliness in nature and human nature. Here is an account of some experiences in Samoa which I extract from a letter written in April 1939:

I have just spent five days visiting villages on the main island of Upolu. Our party numbered fifteen and we alternately looked an imposing and bedraggled expedition. The greater part of the island is without roads and inland travel is difficult; it has to be achieved on horse or foot along bridle paths which quickly lose themselves in the density of the bush. A fair amount of climbing is also involved as the hills rise steeply to a height of 5,600 feet.

The excursion began at my far from favourite hour of dawn and so long as a road was available we travelled by motor bus, a fair match for the wonderful contraptions which I met on the roads of South India. At seven o'clock we had reached the limit of the road and I then found myself dependent on a horse for the rest of the journey. I think the last four-footed beast I rode was a camel and it was not entirely without misgivings that I approached this new acquaintance. However, realizing that a reputation was at stake, I leapt lightly into the saddle and for the next eight hours adopted an equestrian attitude to the Society's policy. I am glad to report that in the main the experiment resulted in a forward movement, though I am more convinced than ever that it is through many tribulations that we enter into the Kingdom. The next day brought me the first lengthy experience of transport by Samoan long boat. I had received the stately welcome which these boats give on arrival at Tutuila and had been taken short journeys in them within the shelter of the reef, but this was a two-and-a-half hours trip along the coast outside as well as inside the reef. The long boats are lovely craft, slim creatures manned by anything from twenty to thirty oars. A captain stands throughout the journey, directing operations, and behind the rowers there sits a drummer, beating the rhythm for the strokes in a variety of percussion patterns. The physical endurance of the oarsmen is remarkable. On the last day of this tour, following another seven-hour day on horseback, I had a four hours' journey by boat. The men sustained their labour in a fairly heavy sea with only three intervals of a very few minutes for rest. On this occasion I have to confess that my gastric endurance was not equal to their muscular achievement, but my admiration for their work was all the greater. They give the impression of being delightfully happy while they are working; songs and laughter bubble up constantly.

During these few days I have been blessed with the sight of more beauty than I can ever describe. Palm-fringed beaches, the line of surf breaking against the distant reef, the grandeur of hills, the rich and almost terrifying luxuriance of bush and forest — all these things have caught my breath at dawn and sunset and in the brilliance of the midday sun. In so many ways, also houses and people seem matched with the loveliness of the setting. I have been sleeping at nights in the houses of village pastors; they are spacious but simple shelters: stone floors, thatched roofs supported by tree-trunk columns; no walls to hinder any breeze that might be available, and all decorated — at any rate on these occasions — with a profusion of flowers and leaves arranged with perfect artistry. It is a startling fact that there is no poverty in this land and never a sign of a beggar. What a contrast to the Indian scene! A satisfying livelihood is obtainable with a minimum of labour and the community spirit is still sufficiently persistent to prevent anyone from wanting. There are shadowy places, of course, and it is clear that moral conflicts can be no less stern because they are set upon so lovely a stage; but it could never be contended that Samoans are driven to sin by the pressure of poverty. Indeed, I am inclined to think that the pressure comes from the opposite direction. I have wondered more than once this week whether a reformation will arise in the Samoan Church except by way of an ascetic movement.

One of the qualifications for this job should be the

possession of a cast iron or aluminium stomach. On behalf of the Society I have sat in state while there have been laid at my feet whole roast pigs, ducks, chickens, pigeons, lobsters, crabs, coconuts, yams, taro, bananas, and other objects passing description. It is this frequent sight of means to do ill deeds that has nearly made ill deeds done. And of course I have already acquired facility in drinking kava with the appropriate gesture and sitting patiently through the elaborate procedure by which Chiefs, High Chiefs, and Talking Chiefs maintain the social niceties and dispense Samoan courtesy. All my visits to villages have begun with this ceremonial welcome on behalf of the whole community, and it has been interesting to note how often the leading chiefs are also deacons in the local Church. On one occasion I was given the rare distinction of 'King's kava', an elaboration of the usual ceremony in a form traditionally reserved for royalty. High Chiefs served as my cup-bearer and bodyguard, and fifty picked youths of chiefly extraction assisted in the preparation of the kava. The colour and pageantry of the scene were very stirring.

A propos my gastric timidity, there was a day when my Samoan guide and mentor, fearing that I should become so thin as to merit contempt in a culture which associated comfortable contours with authority, arranged in advance for a private repast just before the ceremonial feast. In a pastor's house, set out on a fair white linen cloth, there was a European meal — fish, sundry meats, and sweets of various kinds. In the middle of a sub-tropical afternoon these were preceded by hot soup and followed by a steamed pudding and a toasted savoury. Various soft drinks were offered, tea and coffee were placed before me, and the climax came when my dear hostess said, 'Now may I make you a cup of cocoa?' I am still alive, partly because, thanks to another happy custom of the Samoans, I could share these viands with the attendant company while toying with them with unfeigned appreciation. I asked my young attendant at table what prompted such a menu. She replied that she had once been in service with a European family so, she added, 'I come on the table and know to serve how.' 'Are you married?' I asked.

61

'Yes,' she said, 'And I have an only child — twins.' The most searching moment of that day was my discovery that the white bread which accompanied the meal was there because shortly after dawn a Samoan boy had walked and run the fifteen miles into Apia to buy shop bread, and then run and walked the fifteen miles back for my satisfaction. I knew how King David felt when water was brought to him from the well at Bethlehem.

'The history of Samoa is the history of the London Missionary Society', so wrote a Government official in 1915.[7] It was through the Society's missionaries that the language was reduced to writing, schools maintained, teachers and an indigenous ministry trained, and a church founded which for many generations was the greatest social force in the Islands. There were aspects of these achievements which can now be criticized with some validity, and not all the fruits of it have proved enduring. But in its day and within the circumstances and needs of the time it was a marvellous accomplishment in which the people whom Robert Louis Stevenson called 'aristocrats of the Pacific' grew into a royal priesthood in the service of Christ.

When means of communication were far more restricted than they have since become, life on some of the South Sea Islands was very insular in more senses than one. Nowhere did I feel this as much as in the Gilbert and Ellice Islands Colony, sometimes referred to by baffled British administrators as the Gilbert and Sullivan Islands. This colony is about a million square miles in extent but the total land area is no more than 200 square miles. The rest is water. The highest hill in the group is about 15 feet, and most of the islands are ringed by great reefs enclosing vast lagoons. On one occasion our objective was an island where there was no opening through the reef sufficiently wide for the ship to pass into the lagoon. We therefore anchored some miles outside, and I then boarded a frail canoe which, after skilful manoeuvring, 'shot the reef' on the crest of a mighty wave and landed me more or less safe on Jordan's side, cast down but not destroyed. Valiant work in this island colony had been maintained by the LMS; medical and educational work was well

[7] Quoted by Frank Lenwood in *Pastels from the Pacific*, OUP 1917.

organized and under great difficulties an indigenous church was being helped to find itself. The senior missionary was George Eastman, a man of driving energy who expected much of colleagues and converts, but never more than he demanded of himself. He loved a state occasion and when I landed on Beru, the head station of the mission, he received me with a guard of honour provided by the Boys' Brigade and with the dignity of a colonial governor receiving a cabinet minister. He was a great character and few could have exceeded him in his commitment to the world mission of the Church.

War had not broken out when I was in the Gilbert Islands but it was perilously near. Japanese fishing vessels had been seen in the surrounding waters and it was suspected that they were interested in something other than fish. Yet at this stage it seemed unlikely that the Gilberts would be drawn into the strategies of war. I discussed with government officials and missionaries some possible implications of this unlikely hazard. The government indicated that if need arose the few Europeans in the colony would be evacuated, including the missionaries. I had a long talk about this with the youngest missionary, Alfred Sadd, who told me that he would want to stay whatever happened. Nearly two years passed before the Japanese entered the war, and within two days of this their ships and planes descended on three of the islands. By 1942 the British administration was evacuated and all the islands were in Japanese hands, after much destruction of property and life. The senior missionaries were already on leave before this attack. Alfred Sadd remained, together with two or three traders, a hospital dispenser, and a wireless operator. All these were taken prisoner and in October 1942 they were beheaded by the Japanese. On the island of Tarawa there is a memorial to them which reads: 'Standing unarmed to their posts they matched brutality with gallantry and met death with fortitude.' Alfred Sadd was a lad of gay and gallant spirit, a centre of merriment in his undergraduate years at Cambridge, with little about him externally suggestive of what is supposed to be the orthodox missionary. He was from early days a dedicated spirit and at the heart of all his gaiety was a single-minded devotion to Christ. He was thirty-three at the time of his death, having already won in life that affection of Gilbertese and missionary colleagues which the circumstances of his death only deepened and made more abiding.

Some time in 1970 I received word that an old friend of mine named Ravu Henau was in London and would like to see me. I could not recall the name and I was the more puzzled when I was told that he was Bishop of the mainland region of the United Church of Papua-New Guinea and the Solomon Islands. When we met I found myself greeted warmly by a delightful Papuan who said, 'We haven't met for thirty years. The last time was when you were staying in Port Moresby: I was then a house-boy in the missionary's home and I helped to look after you.' The Papua that I visited when this lad cared for me was then the most primitive part of the world in which the London Missionary Society was working. Less than forty years earlier a cannibal tribe had killed James Chalmers (Robert Louis Stevenson's missionary friend and hero) and a young missionary named Oliver Tomkins. During journeys covering about two thousand miles of river and coastal waters, I spent most of my time on a newly built launch bearing the name *Oliver Tomkins*.[8] I was present at the launching ceremony of this 42ft vessel, when the Lieutenant-Governor of Papua recalled his visit as a young officer to pursue further investigations into the circumstances of Chalmers's murder. I visited the scene of the tragedy, Dopima on Goaribari Island, and writing about it at the time I said:

> It is the most depressing spot I have seen. The land is all mud, the surrounding waters of the delta are all mud, slightly diluted, and the people are mud-bespattered although their dwellings are perched on stilts above the swamps. We talked through an interpreter with the toughest old customer I have seen outside or inside the Church. He is the local sorcerer and his leer is something to be recollected only when I feel most strongly fortified against fear.

I saw more than mud and disturbing countenances in Papua.

[8] Oliver was an uncle of Oliver Tomkins who until 1976 was Bishop of Bristol and a former Associate Secretary of the World Council of Churches.

The country contains some of the grandest scenery in the world, and during my few months in the region I met amongst the Papuans some of the finest and most cheerful people, including the most dedicated Christians I have ever known. My house-boy and eventual bishop was but one amongst many of these. Although Papua even then was rapidly leaving the stone age behind, many marks of it in the culture and behaviour of some of the tribes were still in evidence, and the role of the missionaries was inevitably of a somewhat patriarchal character. This was equally true of the civil government under that great and good Lieutenant-Governor Sir Hubert Murray, brother of Professor Gilbert Murray the classicist. Work in surroundings such as these seemed to breed a particular kind of greatness amongst the missionaries. Two of the most famous of these had retired before my visit but they were both good friends of mine and furnished me with wise counsel before I set out. These were Ben Butcher and Reginald Bartlett, whose work acquired world-wide fame because of their capacity for vivid reporting, especially in public speech. Not all missionaries are good at telling the tale; many great ones have been prosaic or even inarticulate reporters. Yet much of the appeal of the missionary movement has depended on the effective communication to the home churches of what the real job is like. Its urgency and costliness, its demands and satisfactions, its worthwhileness and rewards speak most compellingly through the man or woman who is a living embodiment of the missionary vocation. Bartlett and Butcher were star turns in this role. Many younger missionaries could attribute their own vocational awareness to having heard or met for an hour or so Ben Butcher or 'Bati', as Bartlett was affectionately called. Both men had presence. As soon as they stood up to speak it was evident that they were worth looking at and listening to. Both conveyed a sense of immense vitality. There was a look in Bati's eye that was spell-binding. Both men were natural orators in a simple, direct, and arresting fashion. They could adorn a tale and evoke tears and laughter, terror, wonder, and delight. Butcher's hearers were made to feel the mud of the villages in the Fly River Delta squelching under their feet. Listeners to Bati would be panting as they tried to keep up with his great strides along the miles of the Orokolo beach.

At the end of one of such addresses exhausted but delighted young listeners would feel, 'That's the life for me. How can I become a missionary?' None of this was mere play-acting. These men meant business when talking about their life work; and there was something of the same contagion of enthusiasm and dedication – not omitting good fun – in their personal dealings with all and sundry.

Some of the mission stations on which I stayed were still of the older pattern. Adjoining the home of the missionary there would be a school and boarding home, the students would work on the copra plantations which met some part of the cost of the establishment, and the missionary and his wife would be regarded as the father and mother of this self-contained community. New patterns of work were, however, being created and younger missionaries were breaking new ground. One of the most impressive instances of this was on the little island of Gemo, three miles off-shore from Port Moresby, where in 1936 a nurse, Constance Fairhall, established an isolation hospital for tuberculous patients, later adding another hospital for lepers. In addition to considerable medical knowledge and ingenuity, Constance Fairhall displayed special skill in evoking from Papuan colleagues, men and women, a spirit of happy and dedicated service of which she was (and is, in an active retirement) so splendid an embodiment. The course of true love and service in the hospitals did not always run smooth, as one of Constance Fairhall's letters indicates. 'My staff have commenced quarrelling', she wrote. 'But our serious discussions of it broke up in mirth when a young wife indignantly denied having bitten her husband; she had only pinched him and torn up his shirt.'[9] The mission work on Gemo was nobly maintained until the second year of war, when Papua began to be drawn into the conflict. The hospitals were then taken over by the Australian Military Administration and later incorporated into a greatly extended post-war public health service of the government. Papua now forms part of the larger politically independent territory of Papua-New Guinea, with a Papuan Head of State, and the churches which I saw emerging forty

[9]Constance Fairhall, *Where Two Tides Meet* (1945, London, Edinburgh House Press).

years ago are part of the United Church of Papua-New Guinea and the Solomon Islands (a union reflecting Methodist, Congregational, and Presbyterian traditions). In 1973 the Church commissioned one of its ministers, the Rev. Ila Amini, to missionary service overseas . . . and a Papuan lad who forty years ago took the form of a servant and ministered to my comfort is one of the seven bishops of the Church. How touched and thankful I was in 1970 to be able to ask for and receive his blessing.

In this part of my story it has only been possible to name but few of the friends and colleagues who made my years with the London Missionary Society one of the most satisfying periods of my life. Yet one more debt of honour and affection must be recorded. The Society's General Secretary who conveyed to me the invitation to the secretaryship in 1936 was A.M. Chirgwin, a dear and great man and a great leader of the Society in peace and war. To me his friendship and loyalty were deep and unfaltering, and it remains another of the terrible mysteries of life's dealing with us that when I last saw him it was during a period (lengthening to several years) during which he lay helpless and speechless following a major paralysis. As far as one could judge, his intelligence and eagerness to communicate were as alert as ever, but his imprisoned self could no longer articulate a word. May light perpetual shine upon him and upon that missionary enterprise to which he gave himself to the end.

5 ECUMENICAL FOUNDATIONS

The London Missionary Society was an active partner in that movement which has come to be known as the ecumenical movement to which the missionary enterprise has made so large a contribution. It was inevitable that the 'scandal' of disunity should have been most glaringly apparent on those frontiers where emissaries of Christ were trying to testify convincingly to the reconciling and unifying power of the gospel. As a secretary of the LMS I attended early in my service one or two of the final meetings of an organization called the London Secretaries Association. This had been established as early as 1819 to provide for regular consultation between the secretaries of the principal missionary societies in Britain, both Anglican and Free Church. It came to an end principally because its purposes were being better served by a larger organization called the Conference of British Missionary Societies, which had its offices at Edinburgh House, London.[1] When I first became involved in this Conference its members included Wilson Cash (later Bishop of Worcester) of the Church Missionary Society, Canon Stanton of the Society for the Propagation of the Gospel, Canon Broomfield of the Universities Mission to Central Africa, C.E. Wilson of the Baptist Missionary Society, and W.J. Noble of the Methodist Missionary Society. All these were men of considerable standing in their churches and were recognized leaders in the missionary movement. At the secretarial desk there was a powerful triumvirate in J.H. Oldham, William Paton, and Kenneth Maclennan.

Late in life Oldham was once heard to say, 'I had something to do with the formation of the World Council of Churches.' Visser 't Hooft called this 'One of the most remarkable understatements ever made in ecumenical history', and added 'The truth is that without Oldham's tenacious and

[1] The name 'Edinburgh House' commemorates the World Missionary Conference held at Edinburgh in 1910.

persistent efforts the World Council of Churches would never have come into being.' The same thing could be said about Oldham's influence on many other movements and organizations. His achievements were astounding. He was, however, one of the least noticeable of men in bearing and stature. He reminded me of Lob in Barrie's *Dear Brutus,* as I first saw that elusive figure on the stage at Wyndham's Theatre. Lob would lose himself in the embrace of a large armchair; he would be in company and yet unnoticed. But just as the fictional Lob was the powerful agent in the drama of all the characters in the play, so the retiring Oldham was the key figure in innumerable undertakings. Standing beside John R. Mott, who was built for the centre of the stage and the limelight, Oldham would look no more impressive than a junior henchman with backroom responsibilities. Yet his was the creative mind and the driving force in project after project. A profound thinker, always a step ahead in thought of most other people, he possessed strong political acumen and a great sense of timing. With all this there went tremendous tenacity of purpose and personal qualities which evoked the respect and won the co-operation of experts in government, education, and international affairs. I shared the enormous regard in which he was held and yet I never felt entirely at ease in his company. This, I am sure, was due to my own self-consciousness as a novice in fields of which he was master rather than to any coldness on his part. I was also less able than many others to reach through the barrier of his extreme deafness and feel *en rapport* in communication. Luncheon with him at the Athenaeum was something of a nightmare at midday. Small talk at table was scarcely possible and I knew that when lunch was over he would lead me to his favourite seat at the top of the main staircase of the Athenaeum and there embark on the business for which he had invited me to meet him. On the seat between us he would place the large box and battery which were his peculiar version of a hearing aid. Before long I would have to respond to some searching questions. The louder I tried to speak the more banal my stammering opinions sounded, while within earshot up and down the stairs there was the lunch-time traffic of bishops, judges, and various other savants who contribute to the peculiar ethos of the Athenaeum.

However, if Oldham was not good for my digestion or peace of mind, he remains in my grateful recollection as one of the very great men whose achievements and standards are a constant challenge to do and be the best that life can permit.

Of Kenneth Maclennan, Oldham once said that this Scottish lawyer constantly posed for him the question of the moral value of sheer efficiency. Maclennan, who was a valued member of the LMS Board as well as a secretary of the Conference of British Missionary Societies, was a superb administrator, a master of detail, and a fantastically rapid worker. Accuracy and lucidity he regarded as major virtues, carelessness and obscurity as deadly sins. Long after his retirement we continued to meet for a meal two or three times a year and I was always invigorated by his mind and warmed by his friendship.

William Paton, better known as Bill Paton, was my immediate predecessor in the secretaryship of the International Missionary Council. Whenever I think of myself as Paton's successor I recall the story of the schoolboy who had artistic aspirations and took special delight in drawing animals. On one occasion he submitted to his teacher a sketch of a group of lions with the caption 'After Landseer'. All the master did was to preface the caption with the words 'Very much'.

Paton was a dynamic leader. He had been at the heart of the Student Christian Movement in its most exciting and flourishing period. He had brought vigour of mind and purpose to the National Missionary Council of India and John R. Mott had seen in him a man after his own heart. Oldham brought him into the service of the International Missionary Council which had its London office at Edinburgh House and, like Oldham, Paton combined the IMC secretaryship with a good deal of responsibility in the Conference of British Missionary Societies. In fact he became the most notable and noticeable member of the Edinburgh House secretariat and was influential in one way or another in the shaping of the several organizations which made Edinburgh House their headquarters. This was due to his sheer ability and inevitable authority. While his right to take the lead in this fashion was generally acknowledged simply because of the man he was, I found when I succeeded him that even some of his greatest admirers had become a bit restive under his natural assumption of authority. Within the first few months of my occupancy of the IMC secretariat more than one senior member of the secretariat of the Conference of British Missionary Societies took me aside and counselled me for my good not to assume that omnicompetence and omnipotence were expected of me or would be welcome. As an ordinary member of various Edinburgh House committees during my service with the London Missionary Society, I learned greatly to admire Paton's abilities and was much intrigued by his method of working. He had a pretty wit and a pungent speech, and it was fun to watch him and Maclennan in action, often clashing but finally irresistible in their combined operations.

I became increasingly involved in various aspects of the co-operative work at Edinburgh House and served for varying periods as chairman and secretary of the India and Middle East committees of the Conference of British Missionary Societies. Apart from the interest and importance of the work itself these years constituted my most impressive introduction to the meaning and feel of ecumenical relationships. I use the imprecise word 'feel' because, while there are many explicit and definable factors which become apparent through participation in the ecumenical movement, interfusing them all is something more subtle and indefinable. The more definable elements may be expressed theologically, liturgically, or practically. There can be the to and fro discussion of recognizable theological issues. Different liturgies can be observed, compared, and to some extent participated in. Practical tasks can be undertaken in partnership with those of different traditions. Yet it is possible to engage in all this and stop short of feeling under the skin the full challenge and gift of the ecumenical movement. The challenge is against a deep-seated assumption, which to some extent is present in all of us, that it is the others who have to do the changing, or at any rate do most of it. The gift is something which not only liberates us from this assumption but begins to make real to us in experience what we have missed in our separations. I found in the atmosphere and relationships of Edinburgh House something which facilitated this openness to gift and challenge. Not until these years did I begin to feel disturbingly

71

and yet excitingly how much I needed, as a loyal dissenter in the Reformed tradition, all that Anglicanism could impart. Later on this became equally true of Lutheranism, Eastern Orthodoxy, and Roman Catholicism. The need was not only imperative if I was to participate effectively in the ecumenical movement: it was essential to the deepening and nurture of my own understanding of the faith, the Church, and its mission. It was no less necessary for the better understanding of my own dissenting and Free Church inheritance and to the possibility of bearing active witness to this within the ecumenical movement.

There were three men bearing the name of William who, humanly speaking, seemed indispensable to the leadership of the Church in Britain and to the progress of the ecumenical movement. All three died within a few months of one another and each death evoked a sense of irreparable loss. The men were William Paton, William Temple, and William Elmslie. Paton was in his fifty-seventh year and at the height of his powers. He was combining with secretaryship of the International Missionary Council an associate secretaryship of the World Council of Churches in process of formation. Speaking at his memorial service in St Paul's Cathedral, William Temple said of Paton, 'I have never known his advice to be at fault . . . If any man in these last days could be called indispensable to Christian people it was he.' Little more than a year after paying this tribute to his friend, William Temple died at the age of sixty-three, having been Archbishop of Canterbury for a little over two years. The world and the Church are still poorer for the loss of such a man, and it is impossible not to wonder still what his further contribution to Christian leadership might have meant had he been spared. William Elmslie was the General Secretary of the Presbyterian Church of England, and alongside the work of this office he had established close relationships with many of the leading continental churchmen. In knowledge and personal disposition he clearly seemed to be destined to play a fruitful role in the restoration of contacts and understanding between the European, British, and American churches in the post-war period. He was killed in wartime when a bomb destroyed the offices of the Presbyterian Church.

One of the most perplexing moments I have ever known

occurred in 1944 when Dr Cyril Garbett, then Archbishop of York and Vice-Chairman of the International Missionary Council, called at my office at Livingstone House, the headquarters of the London Missionary Society. He told me it was proposed to nominate me to succeed William Paton in the London secretaryship of the IMC. To me this was completely unexpected. I had no ambition in this direction and knew how great a contrast must be evident between my equipment for such a post and that which had enabled Paton to occupy it with such mastery. In the period immediately following Garbett's talk with me my perplexity deepened. It so turned out that before the formal invitation from the International Missionary Council reached me I received a visit from the Chairman of the Governors of Cheshunt College, Cambridge, who asked if I would let my name go forward for nomination to the Presidency of the College, a position which I should have coveted despite misgivings about my equipment for it. It has been an odd feature of my quest for vocational certainty that at three critical turning-points since my ordination I have been offered an opportunity which I would have coveted in preference to one to which I had already given provisional assent. In any one of these situations I suppose I might have withdrawn my provisional agreement, especially as it was dependent on the formal action of the appointing body. I might then have encouraged the other party to go ahead. I never felt that I could do this. Whether in the outcome this has been the best thing for the enterprise concerned I can never know, though I have often wondered. I can only hope that within the economy of grace some use has been made of the vocational obedience which I have tried to offer.

The International Missionary Council was a direct outcome of the World Missionary Conference of Edinburgh 1910. This historic event marked a critical moment in the Churches' awareness of their world-wide obligations and the need to fulfil these in unity. The Edinburgh meeting appointed a Continuation Committee to carry forward its work and it was this committee, reshaped and enlarged in its membership, which in 1921 became the International Missionary Council. The members of the IMC were not the individual missionary societies or mission boards; the Council was based on national groupings of which the Conference of British Missionary Societies was one. The largest member was the Foreign Missions Conference of North America (later the Division of World Mission and Evangelism in the American National Council of Churches). There were member councils on the European continent and in Asia, Africa, the Middle East, Latin America, and the South Pacific. While, therefore, in my new appointment I continued to be in close touch with the Conference of British Missionary Societies, my responsibilities now covered a much wider area. At the time of my appointment the Council had no general secretary, though Paton had virtually become this. Incidentally this provided another slightly delicate situation for his successor. I received early warning from New York as well as from Edinburgh House that, while Paton's superb competence was fully recognized, his dominant role in the IMC should be regarded as having passed with him. Technically the two offices in London and New York were co-equal and the principal secretaries in each were jointly responsible for the overall administration of the Council. Special responsibilities were divided territorially. My regional oversight included Europe, the Middle East, India, Burma and Ceylon, Malaya, Africa, and the South Pacific. My New York colleague – J.W. Decker, an 'old China hand' of great wisdom and brotherliness – maintained contact with the member councils in North and South America, the Caribbean, and the Far East. This pattern of secretarial responsibility was eventually changed by the appointment of Charles Ranson as General Secretary, with his main base in New York. Ranson had served as a missionary in India and had done notable work, especially in the field of theological education, as a secretary of the National Christian Council of India. Before his translation to New York he had been a congenial colleague of mine in the London office as Research Secretary of the Council.

Two years before my appointment John R. Mott had retired from the chairmanship of the Council, a position which he had adorned since he presided over the Edinburgh Conference of 1910, where Oldham was his powerful secretary. I saw a good deal of Mott in the early years of my secretaryship. He was still one of the most active as well as revered counsellors and was keeping a watchful eye on the emerging Council of Churches and its possible effect on the older organization. Amidst his many other responsibilities he continued to regard his share in the creation of the International Missionary Council as one of his most cherished achievements. In 1937 a somewhat slender joint committee had been established between the IMC and the embryonic World Council of Churches, and Mott was the chairman of this. I later became its secretary. Our main work at the time was to ensure adequate representation of the so-called younger Churches in the World Council of Churches and to devise the criteria by which Churches, east or west, would be judged as eligible for membership in the new Council.

Despite this close association with Mott it was my loss that I never worked with him when he was at the height of his powers. I soon learned that although he was showing signs of declining vigour it would not be wise to trade on this. The old embers would flame unexpectedly; his shrewd judgement and his most passionate convictions would reassert themselves and at such moments his eyes, voice, and authoritative demeanour would tell me how much I had missed by being born out of due time so far as the Mott era was concerned. Although he saw the World Council of Churches as the inevitable and right next step in the ecumenical movement and became most appropriately its first Honorary President, he retained a certain reserve in relation to it. He was more of a missionary than a churchman, an evangelist rather than a theologian. It was part of his greatness that he recognized the weakness of using such terms in contrast with one another and that he contributed greatly to laying the foundations on which their unity would be furthered. Yet the hesitancy remained. He was fearful lest any new development might blunt the edge of the missionary imperative. Perhaps my most vivid, certainly my most poignant recollection of Mott belongs to the second assembly of the World Council of Churches at Evanston, Illinois. The vast plenary sessions of the assembly were held in a monstrously large sports stadium. The members of the Praesidium and the principal secretaries were seated on a lofty platform. Behind them, still further elevated on what looked like a throne was the Honorary President — Mott. A remorseless spotlight played on this throne throughout most of the proceedings. By now the great warrior had little to contribute save his majestic presence. Hour by hour be sat there, statuesque and silent. He seemed to me like a living sculpture, and while the unforgettable figure could never be without nobility there was more than a little pathos in the knowledge that he was now only a poignant monument to his own great past. There was an evening during the assembly when the Christian Aid people put on a pageant. During this the Praesidium no longer occupied the platform and that evening – my last in Mott's company – was spent beside him in the audience. He spoke very little, but I caught one of those familiar phrases which, despite constant repetition, seldom lost their power. It was the phrase 'highly multiplying'. In speech after speech during the previous decades of his leadership he had designated one occasion after another as one which would be highly multiplying in its consequences. Even the memory of him possesses something of this dynamic quality.

When I became an IMC secretary Mott had just been succeeded in the chairmanship by another American Methodist, Bishop James C. Baker, whose place was taken a few years later by Dr. J.A. Mackay. I owe much to both these men for their friendship and unfailing kindness and for the hospitality of their homes. James Baker was a greatly respected leader in American Methodism and a man of manifest spiritual gifts. There is a big difference between the ethos of American Methodism and that of its British counterpart. In both countries the denominational machinery is well articulated and efficient and in the United States it is generally regarded, not without good reason, as being one of the most high-powered ecclesiastical structures. A Methodist bishop in America carries a great administrative load and this has contributed to the creation of an image of his office as that of an ecclesiastical tycoon. As often in other circles, image and reality do not always coincide and James Baker was, in fact, the complete reverse of this image or caricature. Gentle in bearing, with no 'commanding' characteristics, his heart was in the pastoral ministry and he was at his best in prayer. While he brought his gracious lovable influence into the International Missionary Council he was not at his happiest in presiding over committees or assembly discussions and keeping a directing hand on the intricacies of procedure. He made many friends amongst us but I think it was something of a relief to him to hand over the chairmanship to John Mackay. Even John could not be said to have shown at his most brilliant in keeping a debate on course or applying the rules of procedure. He could never sufficiently disengage himself from the subject in hand and could easily be incited to become the eloquent advocate of a point of view rather than the dispassionate chairman. Nevertheless he brought to the chair a certain authority and presence which, especially on more ceremonial occasions, enhanced the dignity of the proceedings. A good theologian and distinguished teacher, his real forte was preaching. This had been his gift in his early years as one of the 'Wee Frees' in Scotland. It won him renown in Latin America and Spain where his mastery of Spanish and love of its lyrical powers made him one of the best Spanish preachers in his day, and it gave its own distinctive quality to his writing and teaching during his long tenure of the presidency of Princeton Theological Seminary. Some of us, in more mischievous moods, took delight in counting his repetitions of favourite phrases or ideas. We were 'to shun the balcony view of life and take to the road'. 'Ardour not order' was what mattered. And if we could lead discussion to a point where an allusion to Don Quixote might prove apt (and there were not many subjects on which the aptness would not be apparent to John Mackay) we could then take a long rest from secretarial duties and sit bemused by the rolling periods. To me John Mackay's companionship was always inspiring and ennobling. Though never one of his students I remain a grateful disciple.

The art of chairmanship has always intrigued me. At its best it makes not only for the efficient and purposeful course of proceedings; it can – indeed, is bound to – influence the whole tone and spirit of an occasion. No meeting chaired by Mott could be other than a notable event, even if sometimes the exaltation was a bit too much for ordinary mortals. No meeting could be finally irresolute with Pit Van Dusen or Franklin Fry in the chair. These two men were by far the most competent chairmen with whom I have worked and I found enormous stimulus in their company. Henry Pitney Van Dusen was in every way built on the large scale and was born for leadership. A fine presence, a resounding voice, strong convictions, and passionate enthusiasms all made him a great student leader. As President of the Union Theological Seminary, New York, he brought vision and administrative skill to the greatest period of expansion in the history of this institution, attracting to it the most eminent teachers and brilliant students from all parts of the world. He was a power to be reckoned with in the councils of his Church — the Presbyterian Church in the USA — and played a great part in the formative years of the World Council of Churches. To the committees over which he presided he brought a swift-moving and lucid mind and I never witnessed or feared any procedural confusion when he was in the chair. Occasionally his speed of thought and depth of feeling ran away with him and he could be less than judicious in the heat of the moment but there was a fundamental largeness of mind and heart in him. I last saw him when the effects of a major stroke had left him sadly crippled and almost speechless, yet there was still in his bearing a fleeting touch of the old authority. His brilliant wife, Betty, was also then crippled with arthritis and her parting word to me was 'Why should Pit and I peter out like this? Surely it would have been better to go in our prime.' The next news I had of them was the heart-breaking and heart-searching word that, in order to spare others the burden of looking after them, they had decided to end their lives together. They had for a long time been convinced that in certain circumstances euthanasia was justified. At the end of the farewell note which they left were the words *Agnus dei qui tollis peccata mundi miserere nobis*. I can never think of them without tears of love and gratitude.

Franklin Clark Fry, for many years President of the Lutheran Church in America, was the only chairman to whom I would give even higher marks than Pit Van Dusen in the art of chairmanship. Initially and as a strong Lutheran he viewed the emerging World Council of Churches with reserve and even with a touch of suspicion. He feared the blurring of lines in the area of theological differences and confessional loyalties, and it was with some hesitancy that he came to the first assembly of the World Council at Amsterdam. Becoming assured that the term 'ecumenical' represented not a glossing over of differences but even a sharpening of them in an atmosphere of fundamental honesty as well as charity, he threw himself into the work of the Council and as chairman of its Central and Executive Committees for years rendered a service unequalled by that of any other one person except the Council's first General Secretary, W.A. Visser 't Hooft. Fry, too, had presence and he spoke as one having authority. He could be impatient and — what was often more daunting — he could be seen to be controlling impatience or indignation with an icy reserve. He was a formidable opponent, a subtle diplomat, and skilful negotiator, and there were people who failed to perceive in him any of the gentler qualities of tolerance and reconciliation: yet these were there in full measure and I learned through a deep affectionate friendship with him how much sensitivity, self-criticism, and even self-mistrust lay behind the discipline and the powerful exterior.

My first contact with Fry began uncompromisingly. This was in 1946, two years before the launching of the World Council of Churches. I had occasion to consult him about some details of the 'Orphaned Missions' service of the International Missionary Council. This was the great wartime and post-war undertaking through which the work of missionary societies cut off from their home base by the exigencies of war was sustained through ecumenical co-operation. Between the IMC and the Lutheran World Convention (forerunner of the Lutheran World Federation) agreement had been reached by which main responsibility in Lutheran areas was assumed by the Lutheran World Convention while the International Missionary Council directed its relief elsewhere.[2]

In a few instances there were inevitable overlappings of responsibility and at the time of which I am writing some fresh adjustments needed to be made in Palestine. A luncheon party in New York had been arranged at which I was to meet Fry and discuss this particular situation. At that time, and to some extent subsequently, I think Fry looked upon the International Missionary Council with a touch of disdain, regarding it as belonging to a past that had not passed rapidly enough. I think he was also sensitive about possible encroachments by the IMC on Lutheran preserves. Anyhow, he arrived at the luncheon party confronting me with his most majestic and official presence, and began the conversation with severity

[2] See later pages for more details of this 'Orphaned Missions' operation.

and with that most ferocious glare of which he was capable. My immediate reaction was to feel about as large as one of the peas on my luncheon plate. But long before the engagement was ended I was treated to his disarming smile and a number of those anecdotes in which he so naively led the laughing applause; and, what was more, I was assured of his confidence and co-operation in our further common tasks. I left him knowing I had met a formidable character, but hoping that there might some day be a reunion with the chance to know him better. His sudden death on the eve of the third assembly of the World Council of Churches at Uppsala was an immeasurable loss to the cause and for me the most poignant loss of a friend.

The International Missionary Council was more of a back-room organization than a shop with a front window. The event out of which it emerged — the World Missionary Conference at Edinburgh in 1910 — attracted considerable notice, at least in church and mission circles, and the subsequent world meetings of the Council in Jerusalem in 1928 and Madras (Tambaram) in 1938 each had their own public appeal. All these events have continued to receive attention in the study of the twentieth-century history of Christianity. The issues discussed at such meetings, the widely representative character of the participants, and the calibre of the principal contributors, have emphasized these landmarks in the emergence of the modern ecumenical movement. Behind these more publicized events there was the steady service of the Council as an international forum for the study of the world missionary movement. There was the regular exchange of information between scholars and administrators, and the shaping of common policies in such areas as educational and medical missions and the production of Christian literature. The principles and methods of evangelism and the relation between Christianity and the other great religions of the world were under constant debate. While the main role of the Council was thus a consultative one, its officers were charged from time to time with specific responsibilities on behalf of the Council and its member organizations. There were negotiations with governments concerning educational, medical, and other social programmes in colonial territories. At one time a special study was made of the opium problem in the

Far East and officers of the Council worked closely with the International Opium Commission. With the opening up of the copper mines in what was then Northern Rhodesia (Zambia) there were negotiations with the mining companies regarding labour and housing conditions, including the special problem of migrant labour. When I took over the secretary-ship in London in 1944 the Council was looking ahead towards a post-war period and trying to envisage the special needs of churches and missions in the years of reconstruction. In the meantime the 'Orphaned Missions' programme had become all-absorbing. It is worth recalling the origin of this enterprise.

During the First World War German missions were expelled from territories under the control of the Allied powers. This affected chiefly the Gossner and Leipzig missions in India and the Basel mission (part Swiss, part German) in India, the Cameroons, and the Gold Coast. There was in existence at this time the Continuation Committee of the Edinburgh Conference of 1910. Under the aegis of this Committee there was created an Emergency Committee of Co-operating Missions which undertook the care of the German work. British, French, and American missions raised funds to make this possible, and seconded workers to take the place of repatriated or interned Germans. This service culminated in a further achievement during the tortuous post-war procedures which resulted in the Treaty of Versailles. Under this treaty German property in Germany's former colonial territories became liable for sequestration in part payment of reparations which the Allies exacted from Germany. The property included buildings, estates, and plantations previously owned and operated by the German missions. Thanks to the persistent efforts of J.H. Oldham and his colleagues a clause was inserted in the Treaty of Versailles exempting mission property from sequestration. The property could not immediately be restored to the German missions but in territory under British control the British Colonial Office and the Government of India agreed to the creation of two trusts — the Commonwealth Trust Limited and the Commonwealth Education and Welfare Trust. The former was responsible for managing on a commercial basis certain industrial enterprises which had been run by the missions. These included factories

81

in Malabar where the famous Malabar tiles and khaki cloth were manufactured, and cocoa plantations in the Gold Coast. The Trust Company was allowed to retain up to five per cent of the profits on the industries. Any profits beyond this were to be handed to the second trust — the Commonwealth Welfare and Education Trust. This was made responsible for applying the money to purposes in line with the original work of the missions. I was a member of the trust for some years and it was gratifying to be able to make substantial grants towards medical, educational, and other services which were still being carried on in trust for the German missions. Some of my fellow-trustees were city financiers whose commitment to the aims of the missions was as keen as that of any other member of the trust.

During the Second World War this kind of international co-operation assumed larger proportions. This time it was not only the German missions that were affected. With the German occupation of France, Holland, Norway, and Denmark an enormous volume of missionary activity in various parts of the word was cut off from its home base. In the summer of 1939, some months before the outbreak of war, recalling the experiences of 1914 to 1918 John R. Mott, as Chairman of the International Missionary Council, and A.L. Warnshuis, the American secretary, conferred with German and other missionary leaders in Berlin and worked out a plan for safeguarding missionary work in the likely event of another war. It was soon necessary to put this into operation and to call on missions and churches throughout the world to provide the necessary money and personnel. The administration of such a programme across national frontiers in wartime was a most complex operation, yet this supra-national service was sustained for very many years. It proved to be a distinctive contribution to the later task of inter-national reconciliation.

I carried some responsibility in all this work as London secretary of the International Missionary Council and during the immediate post-war years I was actively engaged in some of its most impressive consequences. At this stage it was not only the maintenance of historic work that was required. A more intricate problem was that of the post-war status of the German missions. Would the Government of India, for example, welcome the renewal of German activity in India? Would the British Colonial Office have any objection to the return of Germans to Tanganyika? What would be the attitude of the British Government as the mandatory power in Palestine to the resumption by German organizations of large-scale activity in the Middle East? To discuss such questions as these and to negotiate with the governments concerned I paid visits in the 1940s to the Middle East and to various European countries. While the war was still on I went to Sweden (with the assistance of the British Foreign Office and the Royal Air Force) to confer with missionary leaders. Immediately after the war, in addition to consultations with my colleagues in Switzerland and the United States, I visited Norway, Sweden and Denmark, Germany, Holland, and France. I also spent some time in the Middle East where I visited German missionaries who were still interned in Palestine. In interviews with the Chief Secretary and other officials I sought to hasten arrangements for the release of the internees and for a settlement of problems connected with the ownership of German mission property and the future of the German work.[3]

Of all these visits the wartime one to Sweden had the most dramatic quality. It was a curious experience, after years of black-out and blitz in London, to find myself in a neutral country with lights blazing and shops well stocked. It seemed still more unreal when, at lunch with one of my hosts, there came a telephone call from Berlin. Sweden's neutrality made it possible for contacts to be maintained with Germany as well as with the occupied countries Norway, Denmark, France, and Holland. I was thus able to get up to date with the experience and thinking of the European missionary leaders on both sides of the battle lines. This — my first visit to Sweden — greatly warmed my heart and impressed me immensely with the character and calibre of the Scandinavian Christian leadership. Nathan Söderblom, Archbishop of Sweden, had died but I was able to meet his widow, a great and accomplished lady. Her husband had been one of the foremost pioneers in the ecumenical movement and was

[3] See further in Chapter 7 for a fuller account of my visits to the Middle East.

mainly instrumental in the creation of the Universal Christian Conference on Life and Work which became a component part of the World Council of Churches.

I was fortunate at this time to be given the friendship of Professor Knut Westman, in his day one of the most highly esteemed European 'missiologists'. It was during this visit that I first heard of Bengt Sundkler, a young Lutheran missionary in Tanganyika and the author of an exciting book on the Bantu prophets. Later on I had a hand in securing Sundkler's services as secretary of the International Missionary Council, and was greatly enriched by his colleagueship before he returned to Africa as Bishop of Central Tanganyika. He later succeeded to Westman's professorial chair in Uppsala.

This wartime introduction to the Swedish missions was also memorable for contacts I made with leaders of the Svenska Missionsförbundet, commonly known as the Swedish Covenant Church. This is the largest of the Free Churches in Sweden. Its polity closely resembles that of British Congregationalism, and it has always been renowned for the extent and quality of its world-wide service. Out of all proportion to its numbers it has also contributed greatly to the public life of Sweden.

The most critical and delicate of these wartime and postwar journeys took me to Germany, Holland, and Switzerland for some private discussions on the future of the German missions. There had been rumours that during the years leading up to the war German missionaries had knowingly, as well as sometimes unwittingly, been used by the Hitler regime for its own ends. Had the missions, in fact, been acquiescing in Nazism and all for which it stood, as a large part of the German Church had done? Or could they be numbered with those who resisted Hitler through the witness of the Confessing Church in Germany? The demarcation lines might never be capable of being drawn precisely but the main difference was clear and fundamental. My involvement in this question was occasioned by the deep uneasiness felt by certain Swiss and Dutch Christian leaders. The Basel Mission had its headquarters and main direction in Switzerland, but it owed a lot of its support in money and missionary personnel to the German Churches and this support was evoked and led by German officers of the Mission. The most influential of these was a man for whom I developed a great affection — Prälat Karl Hartenstein of Stuttgart, who enjoyed a high reputation as theologian and pastor. Even before the war, however, relationships had become strained between Hartenstein and the principal director of the Basel Mission in Switzerland, Pastor Alfons Koechlin, one of the pioneers in the ecumenical movement and a man of great influence in Switzerland and elsewhere. I had a personal link with Koechlin because for a time he had studied at Mansfield College. Koechlin and others felt strongly that this question of German missionary integrity would have to be brought into the open before there could be any genuine resumption of fellowship and co-operation in missionary work. Outside Switzerland this view was passionately shared by Professor Hendrik Kraemer of Leiden, who had suffered under the German occupation of Holland. As a result of all this I attended a number of small consultations which included Koechlin, Kraemer, Hartenstein, Walter Freytag of Hamburg, Carl Ihmels of Leipzig, Siegfried Knak of the Berlin Mission, and Hans Lokies of the Gossner Mission. With me were Dr Frederik Schiotz of the American Lutheran Church and Betty Gibson, an invaluable colleague on the staff of the International Missionary Council. Betty was an accomplished woman who had worked with J.H. Oldham since 1917. She had an unrivalled knowledge of the continental missions, especially those in Germany, and was a trusted and much loved friend and confidante of many of their leaders. Her knowledge, wisdom, and personal qualities did much to make these delicate negotiations possible and successful. I do not think I have ever experienced so searching a frankness in discussion in the context of a common concern as I did in these consultations during 1945 and 1946. Kraemer and Koechlin were remorseless in their probings. The Germans were patently sincere in their response, describing and analysing the circumstances under which they had struggled during the war, and they did this in a manner which compelled the questioners to face for themselves questions of conscience no less disturbing. Somehow, through the process, mutual respect and affection deepened.

It became clear through all this that instances in which

German missionaries had gone out of their way to support their country's policies and to prove themselves 'good Nazis' were very few indeed. In Germany itself the mission organizations had not come under pressure from the Government to the same extent as many of the churches had done. Knak of the Berlin Mission explained this in part by the contempt which the Nazis had for the missionary agencies as being of no significance. It was relatively late in the development of Hitler's programme that the Government began to regard missionaries overseas as possible good propaganda for the homeland. The missionaries were then fed by government agencies with the familiar themes about the iniquity of the Versailles Treaty and the picture of a beaten Germany determined to recover its self-respect in a hostile world. Some missionaries received this uncritically and no doubt used it as patriotic Germans. This was true of certain missionaries in India and Tanganyika. Nevertheless as early as 1936 the Bethel Mission disciplined one of its missionaries for pro-Nazi activity. Walter Freytag, speaking of missionary work in Indonesia between 1934 and 1939, deplored the missionaries' ignorance of the real situation in Germany. When he arrived in Indonesia during this period the older missionaries, he said, 'were shocked by the news I brought them. The ground fell under their feet.' In 1937 the Rhenish Mission sent out a newly appointed missionary whom his colleagues discovered to have been a Party leader. They immediately wrote to the Mission in protest and urged that no new appointment should be made without testing the candidate's political views. As the tragedy of the 1930s developed some of the missionary leaders in Germany, notably Ihmels of the Leipzig Mission, and Lokies of the Gossner Mission, allied themselves with the Confessing Church and suffered accordingly.

It is not difficult to understand that in the first flush of Germany's recovery of power in the middle 1930s, many Germans — like some British politicians — regarded Hitler as a deliverer from depression. As Hartenstein confessed in our conversation at Rheinfelden in 1946:

National recovery under Hitler seemed miraculous and we interpreted this in a religious sense. We were too ready to accept national and economic recovery as a sign of spiritual recovery. We were wrong in failing to demand of our missionaries an explicit choice between membership of the Mission and membership of the Nazi Party. We confess and have learned.

Speaking of the same period, Freytag said: 'The trouble with some of our pietist missions has been not wrong theology but no theology.' Himself one of the most courageous critics of the complacency and blindness of some of the missionaries, Freytag said in one of the final sessions of the Rheinfelden conversation:

> We can give you no guarantee that we shall not again be carried away by our nationalistic demon. We are not sure of ourselves. We only know that we want to live in greater fidelity to the Word. The only ground for your renewing co-operation with us is your confidence not in us but in the power of Christ to hold us. The doors of our present spiritual prison must be opened soon or spiritually we die.

In the great debate on the position of the German Churches during the war, a historic moment came in October 1945 when a group of German Church leaders issued a statement which became known as 'The Stuttgart Declaration'.[4] The occasion was a meeting in Stuttgart of the Council of the German Evangelical Church (E.K.D.), which was attended by a delegation from the World Council of Churches 'in process of formation'. The German leaders included Martin Niemöller, Hans Asmussen, Wilhelm Niesel, Hanns Lilje (later Bishop of Hanover), Bishop Theophil Wurm, Bishop Otto Dibelius, and Bishop Hans Meiser. The World Council delegation included Visser 't Hooft, George Bell, Bishop of Chichester, Gordon Rupp, Samuel Macrae Cavert, Hendrik Kraemer, Alfons Koechlin, Pierre Maury, Stewart Herman, and S.C. Michelfelder. The statement said:

> We know ourselves to be one with our people in a great company of suffering and in a great solidarity of guilt. With great pain do we say: Through us endless suffering

---

[4] For a full account of the Stuttgart meeting, see *The Rebirth of the German Church* by Stewart Herman, with an Introduction by Martin Niemöller (SCM Press 1946).

has been brought to many peoples and countries. What we have often borne a witness to before our congregations, that we now declare in the name of the whole Church. True, we have struggled for many years in the name of Jesus Christ against a spirit which found its terrible expression in the National-Socialist regime of violence, but we accuse ourselves for not witnessing more courageously, for not loving more ardently.

Now a new beginning is to be made in our Churches. Grounded in the Holy Scriptures, directed with all earnestness toward the only Lord of the Church, they now proceed to cleanse themselves from influences alien to the faith and to set themselves in order. Our hope is in the God of grace and mercy, that He will use our Churches as His instruments and will give them authority to proclaim His Word and to make His will obeyed among ourselves and among our whole people.

That in this new beginning we may be aware of our wholehearted unity with the other Churches of the ecumenical fellowship fills us with deep joy.

We hope in God that through the common service of the Churches the spirit of violence and revenge which again today tends to become powerful may be brought under control in the whole world, and that the spirit of peace and love wherein alone tortured humanity can find healing may gain the victory.

In November 1945, a month after the Stuttgart meeting, there was a meeting of the German Missionary Council in Hermannsburg to which a representative of the International Missionary Council was invited. I was in America at that time and, unfortunately for me, I could not be free to go to Hermannsburg. My place was taken by Professor Godfrey Phillips of the Selly Oak Colleges (whom I had succeeded as Foreign Secretary of the London Missionary Society). Phillips was gratefully remembered by the Germans for the part he had played as a missionary in India during the First World War in connection with the earlier help which the International Missionary Council had given to the European missions. At this Hermannsburg meeting Phillips suggested that renewal of co-operation could be made easier if the German missionary leaders could identify themselves explicitly with the Stuttgart Declaration, but this proposal was resisted. The Germans contended that the Declaration was 'made by one group of Christians to another in order to remove a spiritual obstacle to fellowship'. It had, however, been publicized by the radio in Germany and Britain under the slogan 'German Churches accept War Guilt'. This produced a wave of public indignation in Germany, even — so it was said — amongst some of the strongest opponents of Nazism. Consequently, although the missionary leaders could individually identify themselves with the Declaration, they were not able to commit their societies to it. By the end of the Hermannsburg meeting, however, it was agreed that a statement should be made, not for general publication but for limited circulation to members of the International Missionary Council's main committee. This statement which reads as follows, bore the personal signatures of eight missionary leaders including D.S. Knak, Walter Freytag, Carl Ihmels, and G. Renkewitz:

> Looking back over the last few years we see that the members of the Church of Jesus Christ are inextricably involved in the experience of their nations. They can neither place themselves above their nations nor hold themselves apart from the guilt in which their nations are entangled. Therefore we wish to say to our brethren in the other missions that we feel as a heavy burden the guilt of our nation which is our guilt too, and we know that new life and new fellowship is only possible — but *is* possible — through forgiveness of sins and the constant living under the forgiveness of God.

I know no better comments on this whole series of endeavours to reach reconciliation in truth than words spoken by two of the World Council representatives in the Stuttgart meeting.[5] Just before the final drafting of the Declaration, Hendrik Kraemer said:

> There is no hatred towards the Germans in the hearts of Christians in Holland. Those who have suffered much have

[5] Op. cit.

learned to be merciful in their judgements. What Pastors Asmussen and Niemöller have said comes as a call to my own Church in Holland to remember that it can only live by the forgiveness of sins.

After the reading and adoption of the statement Pierre Maury said:

The other churches will not say 'Now at last the Germans have repented'. They will rather accept the Declaration as a call to renewal of their own Christian life and to the common task of re-Christianizing Europe.

Some months later, during my visit to Rheinfelden, Karl Hartenstein declared: 'All German missions now accept the Stuttgart Declaration'. For me and for my colleagues in these discussions the experience was as searching as it was memorable.

I always attached greater importance to the private or semi-private tasks of the International Missionary Council than to the great occasions when the Council was to some extent in the public eye. Any lasting progress in relationships between nations, communities, or Churches turns on personal factors. It requires growth in understanding, confidence, and respect between men and women in positions of responsibility and influence. There is nevertheless an important function to be fulfilled on the larger stage when movements can demonstrate something of their corporate strength and purpose. In my time the most exciting and rewarding of these was the meeting held at Whitby, Ontario, in 1947 in which I carried a good deal of responsibility. This was another of the early reunions of Christian leaders who had been separated by years of war, and was attended by delegates of the mission boards and of what were still being called the 'younger' Churches of Asia, Africa, Latin America, and elsewhere. The Asian and Latin American delegations in particular were strong and displayed immense vitality of mind and spirit. The bamboo curtain had not yet fallen between China and the West. European and American missions were still enthusiastically welcomed in a land where the Christian universities and medical schools were continuing the role in leadership training which had contributed so much to the new China. Some exceedingly able Chinese leaders were amongst the wisest and most engaging participants in the Whitby discussions. One of these was T.C. Chao, theologian, poet and mystic, and a man of acute discernment. There was the Methodist bishop, W.Y. Chen, the Anglican bishop Robin Chen, and a lively young youth leader named George Wu. George was the only man who, to my knowledge, ever shook the imperturbability of John R. Mott when Mott was wielding authority as a presiding officer. The occasion was the earlier post-war reunion in Geneva in 1946. A great public meeting was in progress with Mott's commanding hand on the proceedings. A number of five-minute speeches were to be given by representatives of different countries, each being followed by a three-minute question period. George Wu spent his five minutes rattling off words at about two hundred a minute and the audience was spellbound. Mott, however, was keeping time. Precisely at the fifth minute he stood up, put his hand on Wu's shoulder and affectionately but firmly compelled him to sit down. He then said, 'It's wonderful how much our friend has managed to put into five minutes. Now who will ask a question?' The audience included the American Henry Smith Leiper, a delightful wag as well as a great contributor to the World Council's process of formation. In a flash Leiper responded to Mott's invitation by saying, 'I'd like to ask Mr Wu what he would have said if he'd had more time', whereupon Wu jumped to his feet again and resumed his oration at an even greater speed. Mott recovered eventually but was visibly shaken.

The theme of the Whitby meeting was 'Christian Witness in a Revolutionary World'. Such phrases have since become hackneyed but in the immediate post-war situation they were apt and challenging. Similarly, the phrase 'World in Ferment' as a description of the contemporary scene which we tried to appraise was a reminder that the Christian movement was heading for even stormier times than hitherto. As the authors of the popular report of the meeting wrote:

There was no blinking of the grim facts of our tragic age. These were faced in all their starkness. Coming from almost all parts of the world, as the delegates did, many

91

from lands devastated by war and some with recent experience of concentration camps and prisons, they knew all too well those phases of our age that for many of their contemporaries spell frustration and despair. Yet at Whitby was a high sense of adventure and undaunted hope . . . The conference was marked by resolute plans for giving the Gospel to the entire world. The evangelization of the world in this generation, not many years before regarded as an obsolete shibboleth, was declared to be both a possibility and an obligation.[6]

Another key phrase at Whitby was 'Expectant Evangelism' and this was coupled with 'Partners in Obedience' — a reminder that significant new advances in the Church and its world-wide obligation would need to be through a unity of East and West, young and old, in an equal partnership and a common task.

The phrase 'Expectant Evangelism' emerged during a specially touching moment in the Whitby discussions. Among the veterans who had taken part in previous International Missionary Council meetings but who were unable to be present in 1947 was that great Christian warrior Toyohiko Kagawa of Japan. While we were speaking of him in his absence a friend who had recently seen him told us of his present condition. 'He is older and more spent,' he said, 'nearly blind and with one lung, and he is giving all his remaining powers to what he calls *Desperation* Evangelism.' We could understand why Kagawa used this term at such a time; nevertheless it seemed to us the wrong way of describing a task which depends not on the last frantic efforts of man but on the undefeatable grace of God. So, amidst a clear recognition of all that the legacy of war and the tasks of peace would require, there was a note of expectancy rather than desperation in the Whitby message:

Evangelism means the proclamation of His Cross to a world which is baffled by the tragedy of apparently meaningless sufferings; it means the proclamation of His risen life to a world which, athirst for life, seems to be sinking

[6] Kenneth Scott Latourette and William Richey Hogg, *Tomorrow is Here* (New York, Friendship Press, 1948).

down into death without hope. . . . This task of world evangelism starts today from the vantage ground of a Church which, as never before, is really worldwide . . . . The sense both of a common faith in Christ and of a common responsibility for an immense and unfinished task, have brought us . . . to a level from which we have been able to see our world task in a new perspective . . .

The Gospel is to be preached to all men. Can it be so preached in our generation? To preach to men is not the same as to convert them. God alone can command success, and it is always open to men to resist His will. Yet, when we consider the present extension of the Church and the divine and human resources available, we dare to believe it possible that, before the present generation has passed away, the Gospel should be preached to almost all the inhabitants of the world in such a way as to make clear to them the issue of faith or disbelief in Jesus Christ. If this is possible, it is the task of the Church to see that it is done.

It is never possible to measure the results of such a meeting as Whitby. If some of its hopes and expectations were never fulfilled this is another reminder both of the agelong mystery of iniquity and the need for a universal Church equipped for a world-wide task and with wisdom and spiritual resources equal to it.

6 *UNCOMMERCIAL TRAVELLER*

I became secretary of the International Missionary Council four years before the World Council of Churches was launched at Amsterdam in 1948. The decision to form the Council had been taken in 1937 when war clouds were already lowering. Relations between the German Churches and the leadership of the ecumenical movement were severely strained, and effective contact was becoming difficult. Pending the return of more favourable conditions the inauguration of the World Council was deferred and an interim structure known as the World Council of Churches in Process of Formation was given the responsibility for maintaining such work and relationships as were practicable. Dr Visser 't Hooft had been appointed whole-time secretary of the provisional organization and my predecessor in the International Missionary Council, Dr William Paton, had been designated Associate General Secretary of the new body while continuing to serve the IMC in London.

With the end of the war I began a regular association with the Provisional Committee of the World Council, attending its meetings as a liaison staff member. From 1946 until the end of 1963 I was present, with one exception, at all the annual Central Committees of the World Council and at its twice-yearly Executive Committees. During the last two years of this period I was Assistant General Secretary of the Council. After my retirement at the end of 1963 I attended the Fourth Assembly at Uppsala as official recorder and editor of the Assembly's report. I was thus involved in the four assemblies of the Council — Amsterdam 1948, Evanston 1954, New Delhi 1961, and Uppsala 1968. In 1973 I presided — in the absence of the designated chairman — over an eight-day consultation on 'Concepts of Unity', which was held in Salamanca under the aegis of the Faith and Order Department. All this constituted an unusual privilege for which I can never express sufficient gratitude.

I have written elsewhere about the origin and development

of the World Council and it is not my intention in this volume to retrace this familiar ground. As in all other periods of my life, it is people more than movements that have constituted real living, though I believe in the movements and am proud to have been concerned with their structures, policies, and programmes. If Whitby 1947 remains in personal terms the most vivid moment during my secretary-ship of the International Missionary Council, Geneva 1946 set the course for the character of my service with the World Council of Churches. It was also the beginning of a wholly new range of friendships.

The Geneva meeting was a meeting of the Provisional Committee of the World Council and at the same time there was held a joint consultation of IMC and World Council representatives. The gathering was small in numbers, around fifty in all. As an embodiment of the ecumenical movement it could be no more than a token gathering, but the members came from China, India, and Latin America, as well as Europe and the United States of America. While the new world of Asia was present to redress the balance of the old, it was inevitable that war's tragic disintegration of the life of Europe should be uppermost in the minds of all present. Yet as the days proceeded their most wonderful characteristic was the new unity of those who had been arrayed against one another as enemies. Bereavement, imprisonment, and the scars of man's inhumanity to man were poignantly in evidence, but grace, mercy, and peace were healingly present.

In this company I met for the first time such men as Martin Niemöller of Germany, Marc Boegner of France, Professor Hamilcar Alivisatos of Greece, Hendrik Kraemer of Holland, Alfons Koechlin of Switzerland, Archbishop Erling Eidem and Bishop Yngve Brilioth of Sweden, Archbishop Eivind Berggrav, Primate of Norway, Bromley Oxnam and Samuel Macrae Cavert of the United States, and George Bell, Bishop of Chichester. During the following years I saw much of all these and to know them was a liberal education. I came to recognize the odd weakness and quirk but nothing has shaken my realization that this was great company, composed of people of stature intellectually and spiritually. One of the most appealing was George Bell. At first I found him something of an enigma. I knew of his courage and determination in the stand which he had taken during the war; I felt at once his warmth of heart and acute sensitivity. But I was puzzled in trying to relate the power he had wielded to his hesitant self-effacing manner. He would blush like a schoolboy under praise or blame. He would apologize for a statement or proposal which had not won immediate support, and would withdraw it in a manner which suggested that he was withdrawing himself at the same time. Yet I came to realize that time and again the same statement would quietly come back to the committee and be acclaimed as though others had first thought of it. Strength of purpose is not inconsistent with a gentle manner and a tender spirit. No one could be with George Bell for long, or watch him in action, without sensing a steel-like quality which was never blunted by his seeming diffidence.

In this good company Bishop Berggrav of Norway intrigued me greatly. He was one of the most lovable of men. There was in him keenness of mind, strong convictions with the courage to express and suffer for them, and withal a pretty wit. He was a great smoker and was often to be sought behind a cloud of pungent tobacco smoke, rising from a vast meerschaum pipe. At a time when I knew that he was being treated for heart trouble I fought my way through the cloud and asked him: 'What does your doctor say about this pipe?' 'Oh,' said Berggrav, 'he tells me that as soon as I feel anything I must give it up, so I take care not to feel anything.' He could employ his delicate wit with unerring skill at a moment of tension and ease the strain. After one such episode I said to him: 'I wish I knew whether you are very subtle or very simple.' He replied: 'I wish I knew myself!' I believe this subtle sensitivity to the critical moment came from his own simplicity toward Christ. I last visited him not very long before his death. We had not met for a couple of years. On greeting him I said, 'Well, how are you?'. He replied: 'Just about the same as when we last met, no better and no worse.' I said: 'That means you are still wonderful.' 'No,' he answered, 'Only wondering!' With all his skill and subtlety of thought, his strength in public witness, his courage and achievements, to the end there was in him a kind of wide-eyed wonder at the grace of Christ our Saviour and the Father's boundless love.

The friendships which were so enriching a by-product of my work in the IMC and WCC linked me with many parts of the world, but circumstances provided special opportunities for learning something of the United States of America and appreciating the finest aspects of the American character. In 1946, when I paid my second visit to the States, I was given the hospitality of a home which became the base of the thirty visits which I was privileged to make in succeeding years. This was the Bronxville home of A. Livingston Warnshuis,[1] a leading member of the Reformed Church of America, a former missionary in China and a great man in public and church affairs. Livingston and his wife, Margaret, made their home a wonderful centre for far-reaching service and a rallying-point of good causes. From this home-from-home I travelled widely and was blessed by the wisdom and goodwill of many of the finest people I have ever known — Kenneth Scott Latourette; Paul Minear and Charles Forman of Yale Divinity School; Douglas and Mildred Horton, with Ashby and Kathryn Bladen of the United Church of Christ; Barbara and Henry Knox Sherrill, sometime Presiding Bishop of the Episcopal Church; and a host of others who have enlarged my understanding of life and the gospel and made me proud to acknowledge that America has taught me much about the meaning of a liberal education.

There is one name which for thirty years was almost synonymous with the World Council of Churches. This is Wilhelm Visser 't Hooft who was appointed Secretary of the Provisional Committee of the World Council in 1937. My first contact with him was during one of his wartime visits to England in 1944. After the war we were together in all the meetings of the IMC and WCC and during my last two years in Geneva I was with him daily. From our first acquaintance I have never ceased to regard him as one of the greatest of men. He could be baffling: who can't? He could stride past a colleague with scarcely a nod of recognition, or he would

[1] After the death of Livingston Warnshuis in 1958 I was asked by Margaret Warnshuis and the Margaret Chambers Warnshuis Foundation to write a biography of Livingston. This was published in 1963 under the title *Christian Ambassador* (Channel Press, N.Y., and Edinburgh House Press, London).

break off a conversation and dart elsewhere, completely indifferent to the wisdom which his partner in the conversation was no doubt about to utter. He could lose his temper and then there would be fire in his eyes and there would come a devastating word in one of the six or seven languages of which he was master. In its various meetings the World Council has usually been able to command brilliant interpreters but I have seen one of them stumble while Wim (as he is affectionately known) has taken over and translated with exasperating clarity and felicity. In one sad period when the problem of finding agreement on his successor seemed insoluble I knew that he was not at his best, but many others were in like condition at the time. He still towers in my admiration and affection and always will. At heart he is fundamentally magnanimous and humble, absolutely loyal, and without guile. None of his immense drive has a trace of personal ambition behind it. Through his many years as an ecumenical leader he has been a man mastered by a cause, aflame in mind and heart for its true success, and unsparing of self in its pursuit. He has, of course, been richly endowed by nature – a swift and acute mind, a beautiful facility in languages, a keen political sense, and natural authority. I believe, however, that his achievements – especially his role in the ecumenical movement – are due basically to his theological sensitivity and ability. Karl Barth greatly influenced him though he has always been more than an echo of someone else. He tells us in his autobiography that what became dead-centre to his thought, or rather the living centre of his life, was prompted not by Barth but by a tale about Benjamin Jowett which he heard William Temple tell in 1921. To a young lady who asked the Master of Balliol what he really thought about God, Jowett replied: 'That is not really important. What matters is what God thinks about me.' Wim has called this 'a bit of Barthianism before Barth'. Later on he read Barth on Romans and henceforth he could never escape the profound difference between a man-centred religiosity and a God-centred faith. It was this which determined the dimensions of his thought and the character of his work amidst all the turmoil of the war years. It characterized his struggle to understand the full significance of the practical tasks to be done in the field of social action and it lay behind

his determination to lead the Churches into a deeper understanding of their own nature and the meaning of unity both
for the Church and the world. These were the dimensions
which gave to his speech and policy-making an invariable
sense of what Hanns Lilje has called 'the majesty of the
cause'. With all its fluctuations, stumblings, and achievements,
the World Council of Churches in its formative period and in
what has now become a classic chapter, possessed this sense
of the majesty of the cause. Wim was a leader matched to it.

A year after the Geneva meeting in 1946 I was with an
interesting company in Cambridge when the decision was
taken to create the Commission of the Churches on International Affairs. John Foster Dulles was in the chair. J.H.
Oldham, Sir Alfred Zimmern, Baron van Asbeck, and
Professor Alivisatos all made their weighty contributions
Reinhold Niebuhr and Emil Brunner provided theological
distinction and Walter Van Kirk, then the secretary of the
American Churches Committee on a Just and Durable Peace,
was a most valuable participant. The meeting was sponsored
jointly by the International Missionary Council and the
World Council of Churches in Process of Formation. Historically the IMC had been concerned with questions of religious
liberty, particularly as these affected missionary freedom and
the rights of Christian minorities. Before the end of the war
it was clear that many of the issues with which the International Missionary Council was concerned would need to
be seen and handled in a larger context and with the maximum resources of the Churches. New questions were arising
in connection with post-war international agreements then
being negotiated. There was a whole new complex of questions — social, legal, and religious — posed by the concept of
'Human Rights'. It was therefore decided to create a permanent Commission to pursue all such questions within a
continuing study of international relationships as seen from
the Christian standpoint. A number of men, mostly laymen,
experienced in international relationships, many with first-
hand knowledge of the diplomatic world, agreed to serve as
members of the Commission. These came from Asia, Africa,
the Middle East, and Latin America, as well as from Europe
and the United States. Elsewhere I have written more fully
about the work of the Commission of the Churches on

International Affairs: here I only recall the excitement of the moment when the Commission was launched and testify to my own privilege and enjoyment in working through many years with its remarkable team of officers. The chairman of the Commission was Kenneth Grubb (later Sir Kenneth) and its director Dr Frederick Nolde. Nolde, who died in 1972, was an extremely able American Lutheran, Dean of the Graduate School in the Lutheran Theological Seminary, Philadephia. He had made a special study of international affairs and was a skilful negotiator. Kenneth Grubb, now retired, is a man of great versatility with missionary experience in Latin America, government service in Britain, and business administration in sundry fields. For many years he was President of the Church Missionary Society and Chairman of the House of Laity of the Assembly of the Church of England. Grubb and Nolde were men of completely different gifts and temperament but for more than twenty years they fulfilled a unique and exceedingly effective partnership in a great undertaking. They won the confidence and good will of men of all nationalities in the lobbies of the United Nations and in the corridors of power, or what Grubb in his autobiography has now called 'the crypts of power'. They were dedicated churchmen and missionaries of a great cause, but there was always a boyish quality about them. I seldom saw Grubb without a fresh flower in his buttonhole. I could never discover how he acquired them but no matter what part of the world we were in, and especially — so it seems in recollection — when we were miles from vegetation of any kind, he would suddenly appear like a City gent who had just dropped in at the florist's. In the committees of the World Council I used to call Grubb and Nolde 'the school prefects'. They successfully created the public image of rather dashing men of the world and when they were joined by two younger members of the team — Elfan Rees,[3] a leading authority on refugee problems, and Richard Fagley of the United States of America — we would all be very much aware when the CCIA boys were in action. Yet nothing could disguise their dedication to a great Christian task and they did their homework with a thoroughness in keeping with their strong conviction

[2] To the grief of all his friends, Elfan Rees died early in 1978.

100

that the Church has no right to be amateurish in its handling of subjects requiring specialist skills. I learned much from this team. I loved working with them and I cherish their friendship.

When it was decided in 1937 to create a World Council of Churches, two older organizations — The World Conference on Faith and Order and the Universal Christian Council on Life and Work — became merged in the new Council. Some leading members of both these organizations were also involved in the International Missionary Council but this older organization did not become part of the World Council in Process of Formation. At the Tambaram meeting of the IMC in 1938 the question of the relationship of this Council to the emerging Council of Churches was discussed. The need for close co-operation between them was acknowledged but anything beyond this was regarded as needing much longer consideration. In the meantime a small joint committee of the two bodies was appointed, though war hindered its functioning. After the war the committee was revived and in 1946 I became its secretary under John R. Mott. Our first responsibility was to advise on likely 'younger' Churches which might become members of the World Council. We also helped in formulating the criteria for membership with special reference to a Church's size, stability, and autonomy.

I had long taken it for granted that the paths of the IMC and a World Council of Churches would necessarily converge. My predecessor, William Paton, had been made an associate secretary of the new Council and there was overlapping in leadership, purpose, and likely programmes. In 1946 representatives of the two bodies had agreed to recommend the formation of the Commission of the Churches on International Affairs as a joint agency. In the same year both the Committee of the International Missionary Council and the Provisional Committee of the World Council had asked the Joint Committee 'to address itself to the question of what relationship between the two Councils will best ensure that the missionary enterprise has its functional agency within the framework of the World Council of Churches and that the concern of the World Council for the world mission of the Church may be increasingly recognized.' Early in 1947, therefore, I flew a kite in the form of a proposal that at the inaugural assembly of the World Council in 1948 the IMC should be designated 'The Missionary Council of the World Council of Churches', while retaining its own distinctive structure, membership, and financial responsibility. As an alternative I suggested that both organizations might at least officially describe themselves as being 'in association with' one another, and that there should be some sharing of staff. I sent this proposal privately to a number of Church and mission leaders, and asked for their reaction to it. There was widespread agreement that in the long run some form of structural unity between the two organizations would become imperative, though most of my correspondents regarded their complete unification as no more than a distant possibility. Nevertheless since my first proposal was framed as an interim one, leaving the structure of the International Missionary Council intact, many of my consultants welcomed it. Visser 't Hooft wrote:

> I have read your sensational document on the relation between the IMC and WCC. I use the word *sensational* in a very positive sense because you have done what so very badly needed to be done, namely, to put forward a positive constructive idea which lifts the whole discussion to a high level.

The greatest hesitation about the wisdom of my proposal came from representatives of some of the Scandinavian missions. Dr George Palmaar of the Svenska Missionsforbundet said, 'Your proposals seem to me too idealistic for the real situation,' and he pointed out that at least one-third of the Swedish missions would be unwilling to accept any overt relationship with a World Council of Churches. Professor Knut Westman of the Swedish Church Mission, supported by Archbishop Eidem of Uppsala, regarded a possible affiliation of the International Missionary Council with the World Council as 'neither useful nor fortunate at the present time'. Both however favoured close collaboration between the two bodies. The Archbishop of Canterbury (Geoffrey Fisher) and the Archbishop of York (Cyril Garbett) agreed to the principle behind my proposal but counselled caution, and Dr Fisher supported the device of 'in association with' as a sufficient first step. Dr Marc Boegner of France regarded

my interim suggestion as 'timely and wise', and Professor
Leonard Hodgson, then chairman of the Faith and Order
Commission, welcomed it as 'a line of action soundly based
on the existing situation and calculated to open up a promis-
ing way of development'. Two other responses out of many
are worth recording. Dr Archie Craig of the Church of Scotland wrote, in characteristic vein, 'I think the line you take is
the right one, "allus perwizing", with Mrs Gamp, "that it's
drawed mild and reg'lar", by which I mean that too close
association at the present stage between the two bodies might
mean braking and bottle-necking the activities of the IMC'.
Dr Max Warren encouraged me by saying: 'I think the idea of
the International Missionary Council becoming the Missionary Council of the World Council of Churches is quite first-
class . . . . It seems to me that you have pointed out clearly
the direction which we ought to take.' Nevertheless, he
feared that the title might increase the 'profound suspicion'
of some mission organizations which 'do not think primarily
in terms of church organization', and he added:

> It is very easy for those who live in ecumenical circles to
> think that their convictions about the primacy of the
> Church are shared really widely. I think one of the two
> most depressing things about the Christian world situation
> is the relatively small progress that has been made in the
> last twenty years towards the effective winning of the
> great mass of Christians to this sense of the importance of
> the Church. The gulf between the theologically minded
> and the non-theologically minded is a gulf nearly as wide
> as that which separated Dives and Lazarus! We ignore that
> fact at our peril.

In a further comment Max Warren said with some prescience:

> I confess to being not a little impressed by what seems to
> be a mounting tide of fundamentalism and not only in
> America. I do not think we ought to put it right beyond
> the region of possibility that the fundamentalist churches
> and mission bodies may some time in the next few years
> try and constitute an international organization of their
> own.

In the course of subsequent discussions of this proposal

Max Warren became convinced that it would, in fact, imperil the freedom of action and efficiency of the missions. While he was scrupulously careful not to hinder the move when he realized the strength of opinion in favour of it, he marshalled his arguments against it in powerful fashion. He and I were thus opposed to each other on the main issue. He fought in the defence of the 'voluntary society'. I argued that the Churches were also voluntary societies and I wanted them to be just as explicitly committed to mission. I regretted that we should find ourselves on different sides of the case, yet if anything the debate deepened our friendship and my admiration for Max as a 'missiologist' and friend has never waned.

In 1947 my proposed 'association with' formula was accepted by the committees of the two bodies and subsequently adopted at Amsterdam. Acceptance of two words was not exactly a world-shaking event but I felt that an important principle had found endorsement and I was always glad that the letterheads of each organization from 1948 onwards carried this explicit reference to the other partner in the ecumenical movement.

The needs of the time and the movement of events required the rapid development of means for co-ordinating the activities of these associated Councils. In 1947 it was agreed to create an East Asia Secretariat, financed by and serving the two organizations. The first holder of this position, Dr Rajah Manikam, later Lutheran Bishop of Tranquebar, became a staff member of both Councils. Study and publication programmes were co-ordinated, Christian Aid served both organizations, and all principal meetings of the two bodies were jointly planned.

By 1954 this process of working together had moved so far that an enlarged Joint Committee, of which I became whole-time secretary, was instructed 'to keep under review the present ways of co-operation and to suggest further ways'. The Committee was also told to study 'the advantages, disadvantages, and implications of the full integration of the International Missionary Council and the World Council of Churches'. Two years later we were authorized 'to undertake the formulation of a draft plan' with the caution — recorded by the World Council Central Committee — that 'the greatest care and patience will be needed in presenting this subject to the churches'; and in 1957 the plan which the Committee produced under the chairmanship of Henry Pit Van Dusen was commended by the Central Committee to the member Churches 'for study and careful consideration'. A last-minute move in the Central Committee to defer a decision indefinitely was met by a resolution which included the following:

> In view of the long discussions which have already taken place a decision to postpone at this time would be an extremely negative action. Like every living movement the ecumenical movement can only grow by being willing to make decisions, even though they are difficult and involve risks . . . . The only alternative to dealing with the issue now is to postpone it till the Assembly in 1966 and the Committee considers that this course will certainly involve serious dangers.

At last in 1961, the IMC having already approved the plan, it was adopted without a dissenting vote by the Third Assembly of the World Council at New Delhi, and in an impressive act of worship the two Councils became one.

When the Joint Committee was reminded that 'the greatest care and patience would be needed' in handling this long-drawn-out affair, I realized that a particular responsibility for cultivating these virtues would fall upon me as the secretary responsible for drafting the plan and for expounding it to the constituencies of the two bodies. At more than one point in the process Franklin Clark Fry expressed sympathy with me in a job which, he said, was about as palatable as 'eating sawdust'. I confess that there were times when I felt the need for more vitamins but I was held to the task with some eagerness because of the strength of the convictions which had prompted me to initiate this long debate in my original memorandum of 1947. One of the first slogans which I heard from my mentor and friend, John Mackay, on our earliest contact was his passionate 'Let the Church be the Church'. For him, as for others, complementary to this was the cry 'Let the Church be the mission'. I was convinced that the Church would cease to be the Church if it did not manifestly incorporate within its life all that belongs to the word 'mission'. I recognized that in the discharge of its world-wide mission the Church would need various functional agencies with special competence in different fields, particularly in the frontier-crossing, culture-crossing aspects of 'foreign' missions. I recognized also the fact of differing vocational emphases within the one vocation to Christian obedience. I was nevertheless convinced that all this needed to find expression in the doctrine, structure, constitution, and practice of the Church. This necessity seemed to me to apply with particular force to the ecumenical 'structures' which constituted to some degree a symbolic as well as practical reminder to all Christians of their fundamental unity in faith and practice. Where 'greatest care and patience' became essential was in relating this conviction and its implications to the existing situation. Two features of the situation were particularly challenging. On the one hand many missionary organizations with a great and honourable history had come into existence and done their finest work in defiance of a lethargic Church. There was here a deep suspicion that 'ecclesiastics' would for ever tend to be indifferent to mission and insensitive to the urgency of world-wide evangelization. For those who feared this the word 'Church' lacked the thrilling tones of an evangel. 'Don't use the word *church* amongst our missionary-minded people here,' a Swedish bishop once said to me. 'It will put them off completely.' This attitude was widely prevalent within the membership of the International Missionary Council. On the other hand, the World Council membership included a growing number of Orthodox Churches and their fuller participation in the life of the Council was of supreme importance in relation to all its aims. One of the great features of the Third Assembly of the World Council in 1961 was that by this time almost all the Patriarchates of the Orthodox Church had become members of the Council. What I had to reckon with was the deep-seated antipathy of most Orthodox Churches to 'western Protestant missions' which in general they regarded as heretical and unscrupulous proselytizing agencies.

In this situation I never ceased to feel that my job was far more than eating sawdust. I had to engage in innumerable conversations with people of various nationalities and confessions on the meaning of the terms *church* and *mission* and their inseparable connection. I believed that if progress could be made towards a deeper understanding of what the reintegration of these terms could mean it would be no small privilege to have had a hand in the enterprise. The integration of the two organizations was finally achieved at New Delhi in 1961 when Lesslie Newbigin, representative of the word 'mission' at its best, was appointed an Associate General Secretary of the World Council, while the formal pronouncement of the unity of the two Councils was made by the Orthodox Archbishop Iakovos who had been a warm friend to me through the travail of the Joint Committee secretaryship.

I was due to retire at the New Delhi Assembly in 1961 but Visser 't Hooft generously urged me, with the support of the Central Committee, to serve for another two or three years as Assistant General Secretary. This meant an unexpected change of plans and prospects, and as the step involved living in Geneva it made considerable demands upon our domestic life, especially upon my wife. With her characteristic good will and encouragement in these matters I spent the next two years in Geneva with freedom to return to England frequently and to maintain contact with my own Church as well as to enjoy home. So far as the work in Geneva and its relationships were concerned, these two years were for me an enormous privilege and unqualified delight. The work was infinitely varied and often exciting. I revelled in the company of staff colleagues, in the deepening of existing friendships and the creation of new ones. I finally ceased to be a secretary of the Council at the end of 1963 though I was still given the privilege of returning to Geneva from time to time.

Having recorded the main story of the International Missionary Council and the World Council of Churches in my previous books I will add no more in this personal tale than a word about the general impression which I gained from an unusually long and responsible involvement in a succession of assemblies, councils, commissions, committees, working parties, study groups, and what-nots. As I have often pointed out, the dictum of Martin Buber which was so dear to the heart of Jo Oldham 'All life is meeting' is not the same as 'All life is meetings'. Through these incessant periods of corporate deliberation, talking, debating, and resolving, were we *meeting* or merely running meetings and being run by them? Many of my friends would give a sceptical or cynical answer to such a question and I could produce plenty of evidence to support their dispiriting conclusion. I am still very much aware of the limitations of vast assemblies, especially when they are multi-national and multi-racial, with proceedings conducted in at least three different languages — the language often hiding deeper differences of thought, different habits of mind, and fundamentally different assumptions. Immediately after the Evanston Assembly a group of tired participants met in a newly elected Central Committee. In an informal session they unburdened themselves about their communication experience in the vast Magraw Hall where we had been assembling. In any circumstances such a hall could never lend itself to intimate communication and its inherent defects had not been overcome by the latest technical advances in public address systems. Henry Knox Sherrill, then Presiding Bishop of the Episcopal Church in the United States, protested that 'I have been so bombarded by the loud-speaker reiteration of great words that they no longer mean anything. I want to go alone into the woods.' Angus Dun, Bishop of Washington, said his experience had been about as inspiring as that of a passenger on Grand Central Station trying to hear what the station-announcer was saying, 'and there can be no communication', he said, 'between a station-announcer and the passengers'. John Baillie's version of this tale was: 'At one point I was so excited by an issue that without waiting for the chairman's permission I jumped to my feet and shouted a remark at the top of my voice. Nobody took the slightest notice and even the man in the next seat didn't realize that I had spoken.'

Yet Evanston was the scene of more than moments which lent themselves to caricature. Even a vast plenary session in these unyielding surroundings could not be deaf to the speech of a delegate from the Dutch Reformed Church of South Africa who spoke to a report of the Assembly on *apartheid*. This report was one of the most forthright statements on the subject ever pronounced by the World Council and it led to the withdrawal of the Dutch Reformed Church from membership in the Council. When Dominie Brink told the Assembly that he regretted this proposed action and feared it would do more harm than good in South Africa there was a profound sense of corporate listening and sympathy which became more moving when he added: 'We [the Dutch Reformed delegates] have experienced at Evanston much evidence of what we truly believe to be real Christian good will and an attempt to understand the peculiar difficulties we have to face.'

Evanston was also the setting for some tense moments gathering around two great names — Josef Hromadka of Czechoslovakia and George Bell, Bishop of Chichester. In his last few years I think Hromadka knew that he had won the respect of many who had suspected him of vacillation or weakness during the testing years, and that he had never lost the affection of those who had best known him. The issues he had been compelled to face, however, and the strain of living with them were more costly than most of us could know, and by its very nature the stand he had taken was vulnerable to sharp attack. At the time of the Evanston Assembly the anti-Communist phobia and the witch-hunting campaign were at a high peak in America and on almost every occasion when Hromadka spoke it was impossible not to sense a wave of hostility in the atmosphere. It happened that owing to the illness of two staff members of the Commission of the Churches on International Affairs I was acting as a secretary of the Commission and was responsible for the drafting and presentation of a report to which Hromadka had contributed a good deal. At a largely attended and alert press conference Hromadka and I were the chief speakers, and Charles Taft — a powerful bearer of a powerful name — was in the chair. Contrary to his usual good will, Taft led off with an attack on Hromadka which I felt bound to deplore as being sadly out of place for a presiding officer. A lively storm followed and Hromadka stood it well. In later years he always recalled this experience whenever we met. How far he was right or wrong in particular episodes during his long ·ʳdeal I could not finally judge, but the question of his ·itual struggle was one which challenged my own Christian integrity more than his.

It was at Evanston also that George Bell met one of his most dispiriting experiences. After many years of outstanding service in the movement, including the chairmanship of the Central Committee, Bell was now to become Honorary President of the Council. He was desperately eager that the

Assembly should issue an appeal to all the Churches 'to contribute to a new spiritual climate in which a fresh start might be made by governments and peoples'. This sounds innocent enough and laudable but Bell wanted it strengthened by being carried in person by delegates from the World Council to certain Church leaders, including those in Russia, Hungary, and Czechoslovakia as well as the United States and Western Europe. This was at a time when politically the term 'co-existence' was a dirty one and many speakers from the United States and some very vocal Orthodox churchmen from the Russian Church in Exile were bitterly opposed to anything which looked like extending the hand of friendship to Communist countries or even to the Churches within them. For a time during the debates on this question George Bell was as fiercely dealt with as Hromadka had been in our press conference, and although he largely won his point he was greatly strained and deeply hurt by the experience. I can never forget the moment when after a certain Orthodox Archbishop had angrily voiced his hostility, declaring that he would fight to the death for his convictions, Bell — clearly under great emotion — said: 'I must respect the Archbishop's convictions, but other people have convictions also and I have mine.' I happened to be sitting with Bell during a lull in these storms and he admitted that he now doubted the wisdom of continuing to take an active part in the Council's affairs, in spite of the fact that the resolution appointing him to an Honorary Presidency had expressly urged him to do this and to exercise his 'full rights of participation in the meetings of the Executive and Central Committees'. I told him that I was sure his withdrawal at such a time would be disastrous, that it would bring dismay even to many who had not agreed with him, and that the ecumenical movement would always need in its leadership his special kind of gentle stubbornness.

My last contact with Bell was at a meeting of the Central Committee in Denmark when he preached in the Nyborg Cathedral what I suppose was his last sermon. He was obviously a sick man and he over-exerted himself in a moving discourse on the text 'We are unprofitable servants; we have done that which it was our duty to do.' In the course of a committee meeting just before this event he had said sadly and wistfully: 'Speaking as one with a slightly historical mind — only slightly — it seems to me that we have lost the ability which the ecumenical movement had in its spring-time. Stockholm and even Amsterdam displayed more confidence and efficacy. We seem less able to help our brothers in distress and to speak the just word. Maybe through these last years I ought to have been saying my prayers instead of making speeches in the House of Lords; and perhaps this applies to the World Council.' No one who knew him could ever think of George Bell as other than a man of prayer, nor could we make any radical separation between his brave speeches during wartime in the House of Lords and his most intimate colloquies in prayer with the Lord of lords.

The running of an Assembly of two or three thousand people presents some almost insuperable problems. It is the occasion when delegates officially appointed by the member Churches are required to make decisions which must determine the main course of the Council's work for six or seven years ahead. Financial responsibility for the work of the Council during this period has also to be accepted. Decision-making of this kind calls for a deliberative body in which discussion can be real and fruitful. How far is this in fact practicable where, as in the fourth Assembly at Uppsala in 1968, the 700 voting delegates were accompanied by about two thousand other participants attending in such capacities as consultants, advisers, fraternal delegates, guests, and journalists? Many of these two thousand were far from quiescent. Even those who had no right to speak were frequently vociferous in their applauding or dissenting noises. There is the further complication that proceedings are conducted in the three official languages of the Council — English, French, and German — with contributions also in Spanish and Russian. Obviously much of this work can only be effected by dividing the Assembly into sections and committees, and these provide opportunity for the most fruitful discussions. Nevertheless, the plenary assembly has to register the decisive votes on policy. Alongside this deliberative and resolving function a great Assembly needs to be of an inspirational and celebratory character. Most of all, it is the occasion for the corporate worship of the representatives of Churches from all countries and confessions. Further,

111

there is always present an assumption that a world-wide assembly of Churches should have a distinctive word to speak to the world. This may, of course, be articulated in many ways — through resolutions, reports, speeches and so on, arising from the variety of subjects dealt with. Beyond this, however, the communication experts have always pressed for an 'Assembly Message', a final statement as compact as possible and manifestly relevant to the world's need and the Churches' obligation at a particular moment of time. It requires heaven-sent moments for this skill and such moments do not automatically coincide with the appointment of a committee to draft a Message. Some good things have been included in the official messages of the four Assemblies which I have attended but I have always felt that these productions bear more of the marks of a committee's travail than of that Spirit which bloweth where it listeth. I have sat through many discussions of 'Shall we produce a Message?' Generally the conclusion has been that the decision must finally wait on the extent to which the Assembly gradually finds itself compelled to utter. But as the days have proceeded there has always been a growing feeling that something must be said in this particular form. There have followed long and often late-night endeavours to discover what this should be. In a weary lull during one of these endeavours Hanns Lilje — a beautiful speaker with a nice wit — said: 'In our Church when we can't be prophetic we try to say something reasonable, but if in addition we can bring in our conviction that God reigns, it won't do any harm!' To which Henry Knox Sherrill added: 'After all, nobody will take this as seriously as we take ourselves.' It is not surprising that after each Assembly such questions as 'Can we do better next time?' or 'How can we avoid such and such a mistake?' provoke much heart-searching and not a little controversy. In the nature of the case this will no doubt continue, and each Assembly will be to some extent *sui generis*.

The last one which I attended as a regular staff member was at New Delhi in 1961. In relation to my immediate responsibilities it was important because it marked the integration of the International Missionary Council and the World Council of Churches. It was specially memorable for its Asian setting, for the many courtesies received from the Government of India, for the kindness of Indian friends, and for all that we saw of the greatness and need of that vast sub-continent. It was at New Delhi that amongst Churches newly admitted to membership was the Orthodox Church of Russia. The Roman Catholic Church was also for the first time represented by authorized observers.

My presence at the fourth Assembly at Uppsala in 1968 was only a temporary return to the staff as Editor of the Official Report, but I was very much at the heart of the proceedings. While great changes have occurrred between any two Assemblies, both in the world scene and in the life of the Churches, Uppsala reflected the most radical of these. Certainly it provided more questioning as to where the World Council was going than did any previous assembly. Perhaps this can best be illustrated by recalling the debate which soon gathered around the terms 'horizontal' and 'vertical'. A speaker from one of the Orthodox Churches posed the question and in these terms:

> How should we view the Christian Church and the World Council of Churches? Should they move in a vertical direction, aiming mainly in the first place at conversion, rebirth, and the fulfilment of man in Christ? Or in a horizontal direction, in an activist style, aiming at the curing of the evils of the world, the betterment of the conditions of human life and the creation of a moral order of things on this earth?

No simple diagram or simile can portray the fullness of the Christian faith in its temporal and eternal dimensions. In so far as the vertical/horizontal picture is valid, it is at the point of the intersection of these two dimensions that the meaning of the gospel and of our obedience is discerned. There is no doubt that in its main emphasis and direction, in its ethos and temper, the Uppsala Assembly was more at home in the horizontal than the vertical conception of the Church's task. I was uneasy about this; I feared that it would distort the full meaning of the ecumenical movement and of the Church's mission to the world. Nevertheless I was aware of the necessity to take the Uppsala experience seriously. It signified much more than another shift of balance in the direction of a social gospel. At its profoundest it expressed the reality of the incarnation more searchingly. It insisted that certain ethical obediences in the area of social responsibility are not to be regarded as simply 'implications' of the gospel. They belong to its very essence. Acceptance of them and obedience to them are necessary steps in learning and appropriating the full meaning of the gospel itself. The mystery of the humanity of God as disclosed in Jesus Christ is bound up with the mystery of all human nature. Salvation is a gift as momentous and radical in its significance for man's temporal existence as for his eternal destiny. What the Uppsala emphasis tended to miss — and at times to dismiss — was, first, the radical *malaise* in human nature itself and its need of a power to deal with this as potent as that which raised the man Jesus from the dead. Secondly, the canvas on which Uppsala worked was too circumscribed. In its understandable concern for more urgent obedience within the temporal, it had insufficient time and inclination to face the inextricable relation of death to life, and the truth that if for this life only we have hope in Christ we are of all men most to be pitied. I know that such terms as transcendent, eternal, and supernatural are regarded as dated and no longer capable of being used with relevance to current philosophical, psychological, and linguistic assumptions, but sooner or later, even though the words themselves do not return into currency, the equivalent of all for which they stood will have to be found and used with contemporary understanding. This is a task which lies at the heart of the need and calling of the Church ecumenical.

I was not at the fifth Assembly of the World Council at Nairobi in 1975 and I therefore write without having been able to sense its significance as a corporate experience in Christian exploration and discovery. From what I have been able to read and learn from some participants in it, there was at Nairobi a distinct redressing of the balance in relation to Uppsala. The anticipated 'polarization' of views in the vertical/horizontal debate never emerged, and there was a deeper relization of the inadequacy of any such tendency. What seems to me of greatest importance in appraising Nairobi — especially for the Western Churches — is the leading role played by representatives of the Churches in Africa and Latin America. Many of these had made the running at Uppsala, particularly in relation to the economic and political implications of a 'radical Christianity'. This was not muted at Nairobi but it appears to have been more strongly related to the search for fresh theological understandings. While this constitutes a challenge to the theological traditions and assumptions of the older Churches, it also gives promise of contributing to the discovery of new facets of the gospel which may prove vital for the renewal of all the Churches. This should also remind us that the centre of reference in the ecumenical movement and the sources of fresh creative leadership may no longer be seen primarily in the old Churches with their western traditions in theology. 'The Lord hath yet more light and truth to break forth from his Word.' Some much-needed light on our ecumenical pilgrimage is now appearing from within the turbulence of Christian Africa and Latin America. Are we alert to this? And will the result be productive of a more genuinely ecumenical movement in which new and old worlds of Christian experience are no longer seen in contrast to one another but in a fruitful unity of the one obedient universal Church?

7 *INSOLUBLE PROBLEMS AND INTRACTABLE HEARTS*

It is never necessary to look far afield for the insoluble problems. I have met them on most of the paths which I have traversed. Of all the countries I have visited there are two in which the finding or application of a solution to their fundamental problem so baffles the wit or the will of those involved as to create a sense of despair. Yet no one, it seems to me, can be for long in either of these lands without appreciating their glories and longing to see a better day. The first of these countries is what we knew as Palestine in the days when I first visited it. The second is South Africa. I am not an authority on either of these lands or their problems but in both I have been involved with persons and situations in a manner which has made me a debtor to the persons and left me with an unabated concern for the situations.

I have been visiting the Middle East, particularly Palestine, during the last fifty years and more. Yet there have been more continuities than discontinuities in my experience, and these illumine and add poignancy to the present distresses.

Some of the impressions which provide the thread of continuity through the years are associated with the first few days of my first visit in 1923. Soon after leaving London I met a young Jew who was setting his face towards Jerusalem with a view to making his fortune. No religious move drew him. He was boastingly secular and believed that in the development of Jewish industries through such possibilities as the harnessing of the Jordan waters and a further exploitation of the chemical resources of the Dead Sea there were fortunes to be made by the industrious and adventurous. This youth was a Zionist with no interest in any theological interpretation of the term. His outlook was similar to that of the smart stewardess who, many years later, looked after me most charmingly on an El Al plane. Noticing that I was reading a book with a theological title she said: 'Do you still read that kind of thing? We've finished with it now.'

A few weeks later I was in the home of another Jew, a recent immigrant from Germany where he had held a professorship in mathematics in the University of Berlin. This man also had been drawn to Palestine by the new Zionism and with the zeal of an idealist he had given most of his savings to the cause. He was now living very simply on a new settlement near Haifa, tilling the land instead of teaching maths. His new home was that of a devout liberal Jew and it was here that I first shared in a celebration of the *kiddush*, the breaking of bread on the eve of the Sabbath, which for me provided a moment of worship linking Judaism and Christianity in singularly moving fashion.

Here were two illustrations of what it could mean to be a Jew in the twentieth century — the frank, go-getting secularity of the one, restless and ambitious, and the self-giving idealism of the other, serene in his liberal Judaism. Meantime I had witnessed a third expression of Jewish aspiration. I had watched at the Wailing Wall in Jerusalem where Jews, predominantly orthodox and conservative, prayed their prayers of longing. Most of these were dressed and hair-dressed in a style which to a Gentile seemed quaintly archaic but which, as I was to see half a century later, were to the faithful still the contemporary garments of righteousness. There were almost abysmal differences in the beliefs and practices between these three representative Jews, yet in some sense they had all made their own that great rallying-cry 'Next year in Jerusalem!' — to the Jew an aspiration, to the Arabs a threat.

On that same visit fifty years ago I also had my introduction to the Arab world. The most colourful moment in this introduction came about in a slightly odd manner. My excursion to the Middle East had been made possible by a travelling scholarship, worth sixty pounds, given to me by my old college. Rich as was the opportunity it provided, I had to watch my spending very carefully. In the end, after enjoying six weeks in Italy, Egypt, and Palestine I arrived back in London with two shillings and tenpence (old currency) in my pocket. This condition of things had left me in some doubt whether, before leaving Palestine, I could afford a final day or so in the neighbourhood of Mount Carmel. In Jerusalem I decided to return to Haifa because I had been assured by a

117

knowledgeable friend that living on the Mount in a house which had been occupied by General Allenby during the First World War there was a retired missionary of the Church Missionary Society — a generous-minded woman who took pleasure in keeping open house for wayfaring men, even fools, especially if they were pilgrim students. After a crowded bus ride from Jerusalem I arrived at the foot of Mount Carmel, most appropriately in a violent thunder and lightning storm. Rather than present myself unnanounced I phoned my potential hostess, saying as delicately as I could that I understood she was kind to pilgrims and would it be possible . . . ? Would she consider . . . ? Might it be convenient . . . ?

'Certainly not!', a most forbidding voice replied. 'You've been misinformed.' Blundering from apology to apology I began to talk my way out of the embarrassment but she suddenly cut me short with a peremptory 'Come up here this afternoon and I'll take a look at you'. In due course I meandered up the mountain, the storm having subsided. On the way I dawdled at the Carmelite monastery and stood before a doorway over which was inscribed *Zelo zelatus sum pro domino deo exercituum*. Hearing music within I quietly opened the door a little. All I could see was a monk, alone at a little harmonium. I couldn't help wishing that I had to confront no one more formidable than this gentle embodiment of jealousy in the cause of the Lord of Hosts, but retreat was impossible. I went on to my promised appointment or threatening interview and was not immediately reassured by what I first saw. The lady was reclining in a chaise-longue; she was smoking a pipe and at her side was a siphon of soda.

I was in fact singularly fortunate in this strange encounter. My hostess was one Frances Newton, a woman of character as forceful as her phone voice, well known in diplomatic circles as well as in the Church, and greatly loved by Arabs. She first went to Palestine as a missionary in 1895 and although she retired from the service of the Church Missionary Society in 1915 she continued to live and work in the land of her adoption for another thirty years. I suppose her place was really in that extraordinary succession of British women who from time to time have made themselves at home in the Middle East and especially in the Arab world as though they were born to its ways and wonders. Such women have brought brilliant minds, great physical courage, and intense purposefulness to the causes they champion, creating legends within their own lifetime. Frances Émily Newton, who was most kind to me during the few days I stayed on Mount Carmel, was then working hard to alert her Arab friends and the British Government to the likely consequences of large-scale Jewish immigration. Arabs were selling their land at what to them seemed bargain prices to Jewish purchasers with skill and pertinacity who, like my young secular travelling companion, were eager to buy up opportunities in their transactions with the Arabs. Moreover, these were the early years of Britain's implementation of the Balfour Declaration, that monument to the perils of ambiguity, and Frances Newton was pressing hard for clarifications and assurances which would remove the misgivings of her Arab friends.

It is a sobering thought that half a century ago and longer there were vividly apparent the main ingredients in that Palestinian problem which remains one of the open sores of this war-stricken world. One more factor in this problem had still to appear — the unspeakable horrors of Germany's treatment of the Jews, with its consequent kindling in the survivors of the hope of yet another return to the land of promise. Yet this appalling blot on civilization only intensified the problem already present in its basic and most stubborn features.

It now seems almost incredible that not many decades ago it was possible for leading Arabs and Jews to speak of their common nationalistic aspirations and their unity in a common cause. The principal architect of the State of Israel was Chaim Weizmann, President of the Zionist Organization from 1920 and President of the new State of Israel on its inception in 1948. Weizmann was a close friend of King Feisal I. In his great book *Trial and Error*, Weizmann declared that 'I hold the ultimate identity of Arab and Jewish interests to be a fundamental reality which has a way of asserting itself and will some day be recognized for what it is.'[1] Feisal himself in 1919 could write in terms which now seem unthinkable from the pen of an Arab:

We feel that Arabs and Jews are cousins in race, suffering

[1] Chaim Weizmann, *Trial and Error* (London, 1950), p.294.

similar oppressions at the hands of powers stronger than themselves . . . . By a happy coincidence they are now taking the first steps towards the attainment of their national ideals together. We Arabs look with deepest sympathy on the Zionist movement. We wish the Jews a hearty welcome home and hope that Arabs may soon be in a position to make Jews some return for their kindness. We are working together for a revived and reformed Middle East. Neither can be a success without the other.[2]

As late as 1945 Judah Magnes, the first President of the Hebrew University in Jerusalem, was championing the cause of a bi-national state in Palestine with 'parity between Jews and Arabs in government so that neither would rule the other.' Meantime Magnes saw great promise in a political union of the Arab states 'which would be the corner-stone union in the Middle East generally, arĩd which would offer greater possibilities for Jewish-Arab understanding and an atmosphere of mutual confidence.'[3]

Alas, toleration and liberalism, whether in spirit or policies, seem to have little chance against the enmities engendered by injustice and suffering. The world has always been short of people who could be described, as was Dag Hammarskjöld, as 'the enemy of enmity'. The dreams of Weizmann, Feisal, and Magnes were shattered by Arab recourse to assassination and a Jewish extremism which armed a militant Zionism with the no-quarter spirit of the Irgun and silenced the cry of Weizmann, 'I have never believed that the Messiah would come to the sound of high explosives'.[4] The responsibility for the subsequent tragedy cannot be laid only at the door of Arabs and Jews. Just as centuries ago that little strip of land bordering the Mediterranean was of strategic importance to Assyrians, Egyptians, Greeks, and Romans, so in later years the great powers found it essential to their ambitions, rivalries, and their interpretation of security. Behind the ambiguities of the Balfour Declaration there was the wartime dependence of the Allied powers on services which, in their different ways, both Jew and Arab could render. But the rewards and

[2] Quoted by Weizmann, op.cit., pp.397ff.
[3] Letter to the *New York Times*, 15 February 1945.
[4] Weizmann, op.cit., p.556

promises which the Allies made to both were incompatible with one another. The tale was continued into our own time and the 'powers' cannot leave Palestine alone.

Something of the depth and remorseless character of the divisions so tragically issuing in the partition of Palestine in 1947 came home to me during another visit in 1956. This was in connection with an international conference on the refugee problem, held in Beirut under the aegis of the World Council of Churches. The experience was memorable in all its features, especially the visits to the refugee camps and the sight of families which had already spent a decade in those appalling conditions. I write this more than twenty years later knowing that there are Arab men and women who have known no other existence since birth. I remember the violence of some of the speeches made at the conference. I can still feel the rebuke in the words of Christian relief workers who were immersed in the task of alleviating sorrow, yet critical of too facile pleas for reconciliation made by people far distant from the scene. 'Even if it is morally right to ask the Arabs to forgive, remember that this means asking a race predominantly Muslim to do something which no Christian race or nation has ever done or been asked to do . . . . Beware of mere exhortations.' This was said by Winifred Coate whose service to the Middle East, extended for the sake of the refugees many years beyond her normal retiring age, constitutes one of the greatest illustrations of von Hügel's dictum 'Christianity taught us to care. Caring is the greatest thing. Caring matters most.'

Yet it was a distinguished Arab, Dr Charles Malik, sometime Lebanese Ambassador to the United States of America and Minister for Foreign Affairs in the Lebanese Government, who, speaking more than a decade after the vision of Judah Magnes, pleaded in the Beirut Conference for 'the parallel development of the two communities with guarantees and help from the West to both sides'. 'Neither Israel nor the Arab States will ever gain by war,' said Malik, and he added, 'Israel is a great mystery with profound theological dimensions. The Middle East can never be the same again since the arrival of Israel. When the Arabs reach down to the significance of this a revolution will take place in Arab thought.'

How far-reaching this revolution has to be, not least

121

amongst Christians, was illustrated for me in the course of the Beirut conference by a curious episode. There were daily acts of worship during the conference and in these we used hymnbooks provided by the local YMCA. During one of these worship sessions I noticed that on many pages of the book I was using there were neat little incisions. It did not take me long to discover the purpose of these. Someone had carefully cut out from the hymns of promise all reference to Jerusalem, Zion, and the Chosen People. Pathetic as the action was, I was in Beirut in order to try to understand why people felt like this even in their worship, just as later in Jerusalem I had to try to enter into the feelings of Arab Christians who wanted to abolish the *Nunc dimittis* from the liturgy. How could they sing of a light to lighten the Gentiles which would also be for the 'glory of thy people Israel'? Musing on all this during one of those services in Beirut, it occurred to me to look at the reverse side of some of those mutilated pages. I then discovered that in more than one instance those who had excluded Israel from the promises of grace had all unwittingly cut out the promises of God to the Gentiles.

Towards the close of one of my longest tours of the Middle East I had the privilege of an unforgettable hour with Martin Buber, that noble-minded interpreter of some of the profoundest elements in the Hebrew faith and prophetic tradition. On this occasion I had visited all the Arab states, including some of the sheikhdoms in the Gulf. Finally I crossed the melancholy frontier which then still severed the city of Jerusalem. I passed the Arab sentries at the Mandelbaum Gate, crossed a grim bit of no-man's-land and passed the Israeli sentries on the other side. Then I looked back and it felt as though I had crossed an abyss of appalling dimensions. Late that evening I was in Martin Buber's study. We had talked of many things but not of that which was uppermost in my mind. It was time to go but I could not leave without asking for a word from this good man about the still unresolved problem. What did he feel about it? After a long silence Martin Buber said:

When I was a young man I refused to believe that there was tragedy in the nature of things. Of course, I was familiar with the tragedies of Shakespeare and the Greeks but I regarded these as the creations of poets and dramatists. They did not necessarily correspond to anything in reality. I knew that people could be estranged from one another, that nations could quarrel, but I firmly believed that in such situations all that was needed was for a man of good will to speak a word of good will at the right time and then that which is called tragedy would pass.

He was silent for some minutes and then said: 'Now I know I was wrong. There is tragedy at the heart of things. The Greeks tried to redeem the tragedy by bringing in a *deus ex machina* — a symbol without any substance.' A still longer silence followed until Martin Buber said: 'Is there anywhere in the universe a power that can deal with the intractable heart of man?' After yet another long silence I could only murmur one word, 'Grace'.

Some time before this I had been talking about Martin Buber with an Israeli government official, an erudite scholar and an engaging man of the world. 'Martin has had no following for a long time,' he said. 'He is too German in his thought, too cosmopolitan in his interests, and aesthetic rather than political in temperament. But perhaps some years hence, if someone will interpret Buber in a modern idiom and rewrite the substance of his thought, he may be received.'

After saying good-bye to Martin Buber I walked to and fro for some time within sight of that haunting frontier. Eventually a stranger passed by, looking curiously at me in my apparent indecision. He went on some distance, looked back, and retraced his steps, and with an obvious desire to help, said, 'Do you know where you are going?'

That question needs to be addressed to more than an individual reflecting on the glory and tragedy of Palestine. It applies to the Jews in their need for security; to the Arabs in their cry for justice; to the once great powers of the western world still critically dependent on the Middle East; and to the new economic imperialism in the lands flowing with oil. Where *are* we going?

For over half a century my visits to Palestine have been to a land in which the intractable Arab-Jew conflict has coloured everything else. 'Don't ask to what end I am working here,' said Bishop Weston Stewart, Anglican Bishop in Jerusalem in 1956, 'I cannot answer.' He was showing me round a little settlement on the outskirts of Jerusalem which he had recently built for Arab refugees, all Muslims. 'I don't preach to them,' he added, 'for at all costs we must avoid proselytizing. *I* know that I am trying to help these people 'in the Name'; *they* may or may not have some idea of it, but if you're going to help you must do so just for the sake of doing it and meeting a human need. What the end result of it all may be God only knows. Anyhow, it may be destroyed any day.' There is a sense in which this understanding of the nature of Christian witness in the Middle East has always been necessary. Except in the Lebanon, where the precarious balance between Christians and Muslims tipped over into the appalling tragedy of 1976, the Christian Church has always been a minority in Muslim lands, subject to legal and social penalties against anything that can be interpreted as proselytizing, and with loss of citizenship if not of life for the convert from Islam to another religion. In this context Christian witness needs to reflect the discrimination which Henry Martyn made nearly two centuries ago between 'zeal for making converts and a tender concern for the souls of men'. It is this concern, rooted in Christ, which I have found powerfully and patiently expressed by missionaries in the Middle East and especially in Palestine where, alongside the special features of Muslim society in Jordan and Syria there is the Jewish community of Israel embodying in its legal and social structures that Judaism which is at once so near and so far from Christianity. This is the witness which I have seen in the medical and social work of the German missions whose interests took me to Palestine in 1946. It characterized the involvement of European and American missionaries in the relief work amongst refugees. It has been the basis of scholarly studies of Islam and associated with the names of Temple Gairdner, Constance Padwick, and Kenneth Cragg, and with the parallel work of the Christian Institute for Jewish Studies in Jerusalem. Most impressively of all, I have learned much about the meaning of Christian attitudes to men and women of other faiths in friendships between Christians, Muslims, and Jews where fellowship has been created and sustained for its own sake. Two centres in Jerusalem have for me become signal illustrations of this. One no longer exists but for many years it was known as the Newman School of Missions where an Anglican missionary, Eric Bishop, and his wife, kept open house in circumstances and in a spirit which made it a natural meeting place for Christians, Jews, and Muslims as well as for many who had lost all faith and who could only begin again to seek God through a trusted friend. The other centre is St George's Anglican Cathedral in Jerusalem where I have been fortunate to experience in the home of successive Anglican bishops — Weston Stewart, Campbell MacInnes, and George Appleton — some of the most authentic expressions of Christian fellowship. St George's diminutive Cathedral with its mini-close looks too much like an English parish church dropped down on to alien soil, but successive dwellers within its precincts have given unmistakeable evidence of that spirit which transcends architectural, cultural, and even ecclesiastical peculiarities and communicates itself across the frontiers as deep calls to deep.

In relation to the vast complexities of those Middle Eastern problems which as yet defy solution, and over against intractable structures as well as intractable hearts, these contributions to Christian witness, fidelity, and caring often seem pitifully insignificant, yet they are points of light amidst the shadows and the light proceeds from that Life which is the light of the world and which cannot be extinguished.

I used to think that the Boer War ended at the beginning of this century. My earliest recollection — or the most vivid one — was Mafeking Night when as a child I was fetched out of bed to see the bonfires and the dancing in the streets. Not many years later there came the Campbell-Bannerman settlement which was regarded in our Liberal home as a master-stroke of generous and reconciling statesmanship. It was therefore something of a shock to discover in South Africa fifty years later that the embers of that distant war were still smouldering. Although the Second World War was a recent memory I met people for whom Kitchener's concentration camps and the British burning of Boer farms half a century earlier seemed to be greater causes for moral indignation than any of the recent Nazi atrocities. More significantly, it was clear that peace had yet to be achieved between Boer and Briton or Afrikaner and English in relation to the ancient quarrel over the treatment of the Bantu people.

My visits to most African territories — Kenya, Uganda, Tanzania, Zaire, Ghana, Nigeria, Liberia — have been brief and in the main they have been concerned with matters other than the racial problem, though no one can be in any part of Africa and remain indifferent to this all-pervading question. But in 1953 and 1954 I was given an unexpected opportunity for sharing in lengthy discussions of this issue with the Dutch Reformed Churches. In 1953 I was in Africa for a survey of theological education in the Central African territories and in the Union of South Africa. The survey had been initiated by the International Missionary Council and was one of a series covering the whole of Africa, the main results of which were collected and interpreted by Bishop Bengt Sundkler in his book *The Christian Minister in Africa*. I was fortunate in having as my partner in the survey the Research Secretary of the Council, a delightful young Danish Lutheran minister, Erik Nielsen, whose lamentably early death deprived the missionary enterprise of one of its most discerning students and counsellors. His untimely passing meant for me, as for many others, the loss of a most wise and dear friend. Nielsen and I spent several months in what were then Northern and Southern Rhodesia, Nyasaland, and Basutoland as well as in the Union, talking with teachers and students, studying curricula and trying to see more clearly the role of the Church in African society with the distinctive demands this makes on the nature of the training required for an indigenous ministry. Towards the end of our time in the Union we were told that the Dutch Reformed Churches were about to invite representatives of the other Churches to confer with them on 'The application of Christian principles in our multi-racial land, with special reference to the extension of the Kingdom of God amongst the non-European peoples of South Africa'. Those chiefly responsible for this initiative were Dr G.B.A. Gerdener of Stellenbosch University and Dominie J. Reyneke of Pretoria. I had already worked with Gerdener in the meetings of the IMC and he urged that I should if possible rearrange my time-table and join in the conference as a guest. This was clearly too valuable an opportunity to miss and with Nielsen's encouragement I extended my stay in the Union. A year later

I returned to South Africa, again on the invitation of the Dutch Reformed Churches, for a further conference on the same theme. The 1953 meeting was held in Pretoria, with no Africans present; in 1954 we met in Johannesburg, implementing a decision of the earlier meeting that this time there should be full African participation.

I write nearly a quarter of a century later than these events at a time when scarcely any country in the world is free from racial tensions and when the situation in South and Central Africa has reached so inflammatory a stage as to threaten the peace of the whole world. To recall from a distant past what some would call mere talk on an issue in which saving action is tragically overdue may appear of little profit. Yet, as in connection with what I have written about the Middle East, I find some significant links between people and problems as I knew them years ago and needs which still confront and challenge us all.

The chief significance of these meetings in 1953 and 1954 lay in their initiative. The Dutch Reformed Churches — or important sections of them as represented in the Federal Missions Council — were reaching outwards in the desire for deeper understanding with fellow-Christians on the meaning of the faith and the Church's obligation to those who do not know Christ. Admittedly, there was a strong defensive element in this. The Dutch Reformed churchmen felt — as most of them continue to do — that they were misunderstood and misrepresented in their dealings with the black races and in the principles which were supposed to determine their attitude. They wanted to remedy this and to show that they were not clinging to outworn doctrines derived from a misuse of scripture. But the convenors of the conferences were not only on the defensive. They were prepared to admit others to a biblical and theological debate which was already provoking heated discussion within their own communion. In these later years the critical work of the Christian Institute for Race Relations in South Africa has become known throughout the world, especially through the courageous stand taken by Dr Beyers Naudé. At the time of these conferences in 1953 and 1954 the Institute was in its formative period. One of its secretaries was Fred van Wyck, a son-in-law of Dominie Reyneke to whom I have already alluded.

Dr Ben Marais, then recently appointed to a theological chair in the University of Pretoria, contributed much to the thinking of the Institute. He was a prominent speaker in the Pretoria Conference, reaffirming the position taken in his book, *Colour: Unresolved Problem of the West*, that there was no biblical justification for *apartheid* and that the doctrine was only fashioned 'by fearful men' late in the history of his Church. A more senior Dutch Reformed theologian, Professor B.B. Keet, had also stirred the waters with his provocative book *Whither South Africa?* Keet was a member of the theological faculty at Stellenbosch and was shortly to succeed Gerdener as Principal of the University. At the 1953 conference he read the opening paper with its downright assertion that 'the theology of our Church is utterly wrong'. Being challenged by another speaker to modify this sweeping condemnation he replied, 'I cannot. It is what I believe and I must therefore say it.'

These things were said at Pretoria in a meeting which included amongst the participants the Moderators of the four Synods of the 'Mission Churches', representatives of the Anglican, Lutheran, Methodist, Presbyterian, and Congregational Churches and the European and American Missions.

The Dutch Reformed critics of the theology of their Church were in a minority in both the Pretoria and Johannesburg conferences and they were hotly challenged by their fellow churchmen. The defence was seldom based explicitly on scripture and much was made of the argument that *apartheid* has a positive as well as negative aspect. This positive aspect is indicated by the term *eiesoortige ontwikkeling* signifying 'distinctive development'. It is argued that differences of race and culture are inherent in the divine economy and that a right ordering of society must provide for the maximum development of these differing cultures. *Apartheid* — so it is claimed — is thus in the interests of black as well as white. The most influential exponent of this view was Dominie C.B. Brink, Moderator of the Synod of the Transvaal, who said:

The rise and continuance of separate peoples and nations is, according to Scripture, in accordance with the will of God. Attempts at unification, the equalitarian idea, is a revival of the Babylonish spirit . . . . Even in the Church of Christ, as it exists here in its instituted form, the Gospel did not abolish differences in endowment, nature, culture, etc. between the different racial groups. Any attempt to ignore this will be an attempt to build another Tower of Babel . . .

The Christian Church must be careful not to deprive the whole of Africa's 'Nativedom' of the privilege to make its own contribution to the development of Christian truths. The Native peoples are able to teach us much of father-hood, brotherhood and respect for authority, but these qualities they have already to a great extent lost as a result of the integration policy pursued by some churches, with the consequent disintegration of their tribal life. In order to avoid this danger the establishment of separate churches is the only way out . . .

What then of the unity which we as Christians profess? Is not the Church the Body of Christ and must not all the members be knit together in this one Body? The unity of the Body is a unity of the Spirit. The apostle does not plead for the ending of natural diversities but for the unity of the Spirit in Christ. The Church as the Body of Christ exists here within all the limitations of space and time. Only when the Kingdom of God comes in perfection will these limitations pass away.

All this might have sounded more plausible but for two glaring facts. First, there was never any suggestion that the theory reflected a shared conviction arrived at by black and white in a unity of the spirit. Rather, it is a policy rigorously imposed by white upon black. Secondly, the facts of life in South Africa — economic, industrial, and social — make the policy manifestly impracticable except at the cost of grave injustice to the blacks.

So far as these conferences in 1953 and 1954 reflected the mind of the Dutch Reformed Churches, they demonstra-ted only the existence of a courageous minority of theologians and pastors challenging the views of a massive majority. As the days of discussion proceeded — and I felt this was par-ticularly marked in the second conference to which black

Africans had been invited — a mood of resignation or impotence settled on those who had hoped for some fresh initiative to emerge from the event. Of course, criticism of *apartheid* was not left to the Dutch Reformed rebels. The representatives of the English-speaking Churches minced no words in condemning the policy, and the Africans were movingly vocal in their pleas for a more excellent way. I was grateful for the forthright stand of the English-speaking Churches but the discussions sharpened for me a misgiving I had already experienced in the weeks preceding the conferences. There was no doubt that in principle the English Churches were opposed to racial segregation and discrimination. But in practice, what...? I enjoyed the hospitality of a fellow Congregational minister whose Church had issued strongly worded denunciations of the Government's policy. But when I asked my friend how often a black Congregational minister visited his home for meals and the conversation of friends the answer was: 'Never; he would feel embarrassed and our African maid-servant would raise her eyebrows.' In another English-South African home a very gracious hostess said to me in perplexity: 'I've heard that in England you might let a black stay in your home; I just couldn't face it.' This was not a concession to Dutch Reformed theory, nor was a similar episode which occurred during my later visit to Rhodesia. My host was a canon of the Anglican cathedral in Salisbury. He introduced me to a fellow canon who happened to be black. 'I assume your black colleague preaches in the cathedral from time to time?', I said. 'No,' came the reply. 'It wouldn't do; it would upset too many people.' It was my business and my deep desire during these months as a guest in South and Central Africa to try to understand what I met and not lightly to condemn, especially recalling the attitude of many Christian people at home in England. It must be remembered also that I am recording experiences and attitudes of more than twenty years ago. Nevertheless, at a time when I was learning at first hand something of the principles determining the conduct of Afrikaners I could not escape some difficult questions about the relation between principle and practice in the English Churches. Nor was I surprised when a Dutch Reformed speaker said: 'Our principles and practice are consistent. The English Churches deny our principles but accept a social *apartheid* on grounds of expedience. In effect they affirm an ideal but say it is not practicable; this is a sinful attitude. Will they tell us what form of society they are aiming at?' At this point I realized acutely the aptness of the title which Ben Marais had given to his book: *Colour: Unsolved Problem of the West.* South Africa is one illustration — specially vivid, poignant, and dangerous — of a world-wide problem. It has not yet been solved in the United States, despite brave endeavours to compass it. It simmers in Britain, with occasional dangerous eruptions. What form of society will make possible, without discriminations and injustices, a genuine unity encompassing a rich and increasing diversity? 'We do not want intermingling,' said a black South African at Pretoria, 'we ask for justice, mutual respect, and equal opportunity.' These terms have to be spelt out in political and economic language, and there is no short cut through the exercise. What has been lacking for too long is a genuine meeting of black and white in working at the task, both in regard to fundamental principles and their political application. In South Africa, in so far as theological convictions have determined or supported *apartheid* and its consequent injustices, it has been a white theology and therefore deficient. Is the emergence of a 'black theology', as in the USA and to some extent in Africa, likely to be any less deficient? Can the minds of black and white together come any nearer to the mind of Christ?

One of my lasting memories of South Africa is associated with an evening in the home of a Dutch Reformed pastor who was in charge of a little training school for African ministers at a place called Dinganstaat. On that evening black and white together enjoyed a relaxed conversation on some of the things that matter most and we said our evening prayers together. The name of the place recalls a Zulu chief who, more than a century ago, led an attack on a company of Boer settlers and massacred them. A memorial stone records the tragedy and on it are the names of the victims. My host was a descendant of one of those named, and in addition to the training school he was running an orphanage for Zulu children. In the same neighbourhood there is a group of huts, built in traditional Zulu fashion, which house the students for the ministry, and over each hut's entrance there is the name of one of the victims of long ago.[5] The cost of building the huts was met by descendants of these same murdered Boers. The land and the orphanage buildings together with two farms were the gift of two Boer farmers, one of whom did more than donate the necessary funds. When it was discovered that for irrigation purposes a new dam was required, this Afrikaner left his home for some weeks, built a shack near the site of the dam and daily worked with the African labourers. While this was happening one of the students in the training school, taking his turn in leading evening worship, offered a prayer in these words:

> We thank thee, O Father, for the man who gave us the land — but it was easy for him to do it for he has much land. We thank thee that he gave us a hundred oxen — but he has many oxen. We thank thee that he gave us two farms — but he has many farms. Now he is building us a dam with his own hands — and this has beaten us.

A right spirit will not alone provide political and economic solutions of intractable social problems. But a wrong spirit can defeat a perfect economic or political solution. The right spirit is at least a necessary ingredient for achieving a viable solution, and it is the supreme necessity for dealing with that most stubborn hindrance to peace and justice — the intractable heart.

[5] I am not overlooking the fact that retribution for the massacre of the Boers was inflicted on the Zulus in 1838 and that 'Dingaan's Day' still commemorates this punitive victory. Nevertheless, the more recent act of retaliation in mercy deserves to be recorded and remembered.

'O Spirit of Truth, where wert thou when the dark waters of superstition closed over the head of John Henry Newman, who surely deserved to be called thy best loved son?' This plaintive cry appeared many years ago in an essay on Newman by Augustine Birrell. Birrell was one of the genial litterateurs of my boyhood. A Liberal politician of the Asquithian breed, his journalistic comments on men and books published in the *Daily News* (and later in such volumes as his *Obiter Dicta*) were much relished in my early home. He wrote with a gentle urbanity and a kindly tolerance. During my time in the Civil Service I frequently saw him sauntering into the House of Commons where he surveyed the scene for a few minutes with benign interest and then sauntered out again. His equation of Roman Catholicism with the dark waters of superstition was clearly made more in sorrow than in anger; he must have been sadly stricken to have had recourse to 'Where wert thou?' Nevertheless the equation of Rome with superstition was scarcely questioned in the Protestant and Evangelical circles of my boyhood and most of my later years. As a child my way to school took me past a convent, a sombre building with a heavy entrance door in which there was a curious looking grille. I took great care to cross to the other side of the road when nearing the convent. Who could tell what dark and sinister shape might suddenly emerge from it. It was a shock when one day I learned that our family doctor was a Roman Catholic. How could so kindly, generous, and lovable a man be one of those?

Happily there were other inconsistencies to challenge inherited assumptions. When I was about sixteen my staunchly Protestant father insisted that I should read Newman's *Apologia pro vita sua*. He commended it as a literary *tour de force* and was moved by its hauntingly persuasive style. All my father's convictions and sympathies were with Charles Kingsley in the controversy which evoked the *Apologia*. Yet he had to admit that there were deeps in Newman's faith and experience to which Kingsley was sadly tone-deaf. Years later, in my father's greatest need as he was ending his days bed-ridden, no ministry to his troubled spirit save that of the Wesleys' hymns meant as much as the broadcast addresses of Father d'Arcy.

The change in climate in church relationships signalized by the Second Vatican Council came late in my ministry, though I had long been aware of the inadequacy of earlier stereotypes of Catholic and Protestant. My reading of church history, my dependence on Roman Catholic writers — especially Baron von Hügel — participation in prayers for Christian unity, the influence of the Student Christian Movement, and new relationships between all the Churches during the necessities of war, were all powerful influences making for deeper understanding and better relationships. During my secretarial work with the London Missionary Society there was a certain ambivalence in the attitude of the Society to Roman Catholic missions. Charges of 'sheep stealing' were still bandied to and fro. The term 'religious liberty' was very differently interpreted by Roman Catholics and Protestants in respect of missionary freedom, and the memory of earlier controversies and conflicts in which political divisions had coincided with religious differences — as in Madagascar and the South Seas — was still considerably tinged with resentment and bitterness. On the other hand, in the course of the Society's discussions of policy at the more fundamental level of re-thinking the meaning and goals of the missionary imperative, we were much aware of the constructive and challenging contributions of the Jesuit Pierre Charles of the Louvain School, and of the Maryknoll Fathers in America. When I moved from the London Missionary Society to the International Missionary Council, I had further opportunities for enriching collaboration. From as early as 1912 the *International Review of Missions*, of which I became editor in 1944, had opened its pages to Roman Catholic contributors and in the annual survey of the world-wide missionary enterprise a special section was devoted to Roman Catholic missions. This, and a number of research projects undertaken by the International Missionary Council in collaboration with Roman Catholics, opened up an increasing range of valuable personal contacts and friendships.

Until 1960 there was no official observer attendance of Roman Catholics at World Council meetings, but for many years before the Council's first Assembly in 1948 there existed close personal relationships between leading Roman Catholics and those who were involved in the processes which led to the launching of the World Council. Biblical and theological scholarship had long since transcended the barriers, and by 1948 there was a considerable volume of Roman Catholic interest in the ecumenical movement as this was finding expression outside Rome. In Europe and America there were Roman Catholic ecumenists who worked closely with their not so separated brethren. If as yet the Vatican could not authorize overt or official relationships with the World Council, there was an encouraging attendance in the press gallery of journalists who turned out to be Roman Catholic theologians of some standing.

A major change came with the formation in 1960 of the Vatican Secretariat for Promoting Christian Unity. This was initially responsible for work required in the preparations for the Second Vatican Council, but it soon became — as it has continued to be — the main channel of communication between Rome and the other Churches. Its first president was Cardinal Augustin Bea, and its secretary was Mgr Jan Wille-brands. Fr Willebrands later became a cardinal and succeeded to the presidency. He had long been one of the keen Roman Catholic ecumenists and was a close friend of his fellow Dutchman, Visser 't Hooft. In the course of preparations for the Vatican Council he was frequently in Geneva and during one of these visits he raised the question, on behalf of Pope John, of possible attendance at the Council of official observers from the other Churches. If an invitation were to be extended by the Vatican to some of the member Churches of the World Council, was it likely that there would be a favourable response? I happened at the time to be chairman of an informal group, meeting annually in Geneva, consisting of officers of what were then commonly known as the World Confessional Bodies. These were organizations varying greatly in size and character which represented the larger denominations or confessions in their world-wide scope, such as the Lutheran World Federation, the World Methodist Council, the World Alliance of Reformed Churches, and the

International Congregational Council of which I was then Moderator. After consultation with this group we were able to answer Willebrands' question with a warm assurance that any such invitation was likely to be gratefully accepted. We suggested further that the appointment of the observers should be the responsibility of these World Confessional Bodies, or World Families of Churches as they are now more frequently styled.

Among those who found deep satisfaction in these momentous changes in relationships none was more thankful than the Jesuit, Father Bernard Leeming, Professor of Sacramental Theology at the Heythrop Seminary. He had long been actively identified with the many movements which were making for better understanding between the Churches and was regarded as the doyen of Roman Catholic ecumenists. From the earliest days of the World Council he had been one of those theologians who appeared in the guise of journalists in the press galleries, and it had become impossible to think of this genial and lovable scholar merely as a visitor or even as a separated friend. He belonged to us all. In addition to enriching life by the kind of person he was, he established relationships and used his great influence in ways which made possible theological collaboration of the greatest value during the formative years of the World Council. My own acquaintance with him moved into a warm friendship at the time when he was writing his book *The Church, the Churches and the World Council of Churches*. This included a study of the processes which led to the formation of the Council and gave special attention to the role of the International Missionary Council. With the desire that his narration of events should be as accurate as possible, Fr Leeming asked me to read his manuscript and comment on it. Later on he inquired whether it would cause me any embarrassment if in the preface he acknowledged the help that I had given him. 'If you would rather remain anonymous,' he said, 'I shall quite understand' and he then regaled me with a story which needs to be told with the right Irish accent. In the days when it was easier to treat the North-South, Protestant-Catholic divide more light-heartedly than during these later tragic years, two Irish women — a Catholic and a Protestant — had reached argumentative exhaustion after the Southerner had failed to persuade the Northerner of the truth of Roman Catholicism. 'Well, my dear,' said the champion of Rome, 'I can't convert you but I'll pray for you,' to which the Protestant replied: 'Well, Mrs Murphy, if you pray for me to the Virgin Mary I'll thank you not to mention my name.'

It was largely due to the good will of Bernard Leeming that in the academic session of 1968-9 I became an Assistant Lecturer at Heythrop in a course for advanced students of ecclesiology and ecumenical theology. This was directed by another good friend, Father Robert Murray SJ, with whom and with whose family I had enjoyed associations during my years with the London Missionary Society. Robert's father, Jowett Murray (a Congregationalist, later an Anglican) was a missionary in China in the great succession of scholar missionaries. His father — Robert's grandfather — was the great 'Dictionary Murray', the original editor of the mammoth *Oxford English Dictionary*. Robert is a scholar born. It was during his undergraduate years at Oxford that he became a Roman Catholic and in happy contrast to some other zealous converts he has never spoken disdainfully of his Protestant inheritance and he continues to exercise a ministry of understanding and reconciliation between the Churches.

My period of service at Heythrop meant much to me. Other members of the faculty were as welcoming as those I have already named. It was good to be in the company of Professor F.C. Copleston, Father John Coventry, and the Dean of Theology, Father Brinkman. During this time I happened also to meet the venerable scholar Father Charles Boyer, who was visiting Heythrop; he was one of the first to welcome me to Rome some years later. Fr Boyer was allegedly responsible for a nice rejoinder which endeared him to me. It is said that a young ordinand, impatient of what was to him a lack of progressiveness in the Vatican, angrily exclaimed to Fr Boyer: 'If the Pope doesn't sanction the ordination of women to the priesthood before Christmas I shall leave the Church.' 'How sad!' said Fr Boyer. 'I can only say that if the Holy Father does sanction the ordination of women before Christmas I shall not leave the Church.'

At Heythrop I lectured twice weekly on the history of the ecumenical movement to a stimulating company, not only Jesuit priests and ordinands, but members of other Orders who were also studying in this Pontifical Athenaeum. It was another sign of the influence of the Second Vatican Council that my class included a number of nuns. I was particularly grateful to be invited on my last day at Heythrop to lead worship in the College chapel.

Early in 1971 I received a visit from Father Michael Hurley SJ, under whose direction there had recently been launched in Dublin an exciting new venture called the Irish School of Ecumenics. Michael Hurley was a member of the Faculty of the Jesuit Institute of Theology and Philosophy at Milltown Park, and he had been released by his Order to embark on this experiment in the interests of the ecumenical movement. The School is under the general direction of an Academic Council and Executive Board composed of Catholics and Protestants from Northern Ireland as well as Eire. The student enrolment reaches out to all communions and countries. I was greatly attracted by the nature and purpose of this venture and was grateful to be able to lecture during two terms in 1971 and 1972. My first class in the second year of the School's life consisted of only eight students but there was a diversity which included a French White Father from Tanzania, an American Mennonite Professor of Practical Theology from Indiana, an African Roman Catholic priest from the Transvaal, a Church of Ireland priest, and two nuns from the Society of the Sacred Heart and the Missionary Sisters of Our Lady of the Apostles. The basic course of study provided by the School leads to a postgraduate Diploma in Ecumenics and, by arrangement with Nottingham University, to the degree of Bachelor of Philosophy. Research and seminars are conducted with particular reference to problems intensified by the religious and political differences between Eire and Northern Ireland, such as mixed marriages and integrated education. I found the School's motto and emblem very congenial. The words *Floreat ut pereat* (May it flourish in order to perish) surround an ear of wheat, indicating what the School describes as its commitment to 'the death of ecumenism and the rebirth of the Church as God's one eucharistic people united for mission'. For me the friendship of Michael Hurley and his colleagues remains a permanent reward and my friendships, and correspondingly my understanding of Catholicism, were further increased by visits to the Theological Institute at Milltown Park, the University College of Maynooth, the Holy Ghost Fathers, and the Augustinian House of Studies. It was there I found a kindred spirit and excellent friend in Father Gabriel Daly, whose taste in music and studies in the significance of the work of von Hügel and Loisy matched my own interests.

In 1974 I was invited to spend a semester in Rome as a Visiting Professor in the Pontifical Gregorian University. I owed this privilege to the initiative of the Jesuit Father Jan Witte, Professor of Protestant and Ecumenical Theology in the University. I had previously enjoyed Professor Witte's company in 1973 at a Faith and Order conference in Salamanca, over which I was presiding. Fr Witte then told me that my two books on the ecumenical movement[1] were being used in Rome and that a visit would be welcome if the necessary authority could be obtained from the Congregation of Studies and the Faculty of Theology. This was secured and I spent ten weeks in Rome in 1975, when I was most graciously received by staff and students alike.

The Gregorian University, commonly known as 'The Greg', was originally called the Roman College. It owed its initial fame and influence to Ignatius Loyola, the creator of the Jesuit Order. It became a Pontifical University under Pope Gregory XIII in the sixteenth century and continues to be pre-eminent amongst the many learned institutions in the Roman Catholic world. My course of lectures on the ecumenical movement was for a class of twenty-eight graduate students. Some of these were still in process of their training for the priesthood, others were experienced teachers and theologians who were in Rome for doctoral studies. They came from Northern Ireland, India, the West Indies and Africa, as well as from Great Britain. Most of the senior ones were well versed in ecumenical history. For some of the younger ones it was news that there was an ecumenical movement before Pope John XXIII, and all were surprised at the vital role which the missionary enterprise of the non-Roman

[1] *The Ecumenical Movement: What it is and what it does* (London, OUP, 1961); second edition, with new Preface and additional material covering the period 1961-1964 (OUP, 1964); and *Ecumenical Progress; A Decade of Change in the Ecumenical Movement, 1961-1971* (OUP, 1972).

Churches had played in the history of the movement. I learned at least as much as I taught, and even my obligation to examine the students at the end of the course does not appear to have greatly hindered the growth of friendships which I greatly cherish. Beyond my responsibilities at the Greg, I was able to make other contacts in Rome with members of the Vatican Secretariat for Christian Unity and with students and Faculty members of other universities and colleges. It was Holy Year and I was aware of the questions — theological and tactical — which had been provoked by Pope Paul's declaration of the Year. But I was moved by the sight of the many pilgrims of all nationalities thronging the city and clearly entering with jubilation and high expectation into the liturgical and devotional exercises of the pilgrimage. I was grateful to be invited to preach at one of the Holy Year ecumenical services arranged by the Secretariat for Unity in the Church of Santo Spirito in Sassia. This splendidly flamboyant baroque building is on the site of a twelfth-century church founded for Saxon (Sassia) pilgrims from the former nation of Wessex.

During my responsibilities at the Greg I was housed in the Venerable English College which traces its origin to a pilgrim hostel of the thirteenth century founded by what was then described as the Community and College of the English in Rome. The College has had an exciting and often stormy history in which notable figures of the Renaissance, the Reformation, and the Counter-Reformation played their part. In Tudor times the wardens were usually the Royal Ambassadors in Rome. The roll of residents in the hostel included such a diversity as Thomas Linacre, John Colet, Thomas Cromwell, William Harvey, John Milton, Richard Crashaw, and John Evelyn. Under Pope Gregory XIII the hospice became a college for the training of priests dedicated to the hazardous enterprise of bringing the apostate English back into the Catholic fold. Thus the 'English martyrs' of the Counter-Reformation have a special place in the community's roll of honour. While these were scarcely the heroes of my boyhood or the most honoured names in my Protestant upbringing, I have always had more than a sneaking appreciation of these men who knew that fidelity to their understanding of Catholicism must make them dissenters in England to the peril of imprisonment and death. My dissenting inheritance was born in a similar costly loyalty to a different under-standing of the catholicity of the gospel and the people of Christ. I was glad of the opportunity occasionally to draw the attention of my new friends in Rome to this parallel and to boast, with proper modesty I hope, that in the nineteenth century English Protestant dissenters were amongst those who most warmly supported Catholic emancipation in the light of their understanding of religious liberty.

Merely to say that I was 'housed' in the English College is a massive understatement for I have never been more warmly and readily received into any society with which I have been associated. My residence in the Venerabile proved to be a period of deep renewal of my own faith as well as one in which I was wonderfully blessed by the friendship of students and faculty. Remembering that by this time I was approaching my eightieth year, the generation gap between me and the students was more than slight. I cannot, of course, speak for those on the other side of the gap, but whether in things grave or gay the community seemed to me to be possessed of a genius for transcending the differences of years and for achieving and revelling in relationships in which the timeless things are what matters, and young and old are caught up into eternities that are contemporary. We talked about heaven and hell as easily as about cabbages and kings, about the world in which we live and the world we are made for, about life's delights and absurdities, and most of all about those centralities of the faith and the experience of grace in which is our real and unassailable unity. I shared in the daily disci-plined worship of the community and preached in the College chapel and shared confidences regarding our Christian voca-tion with men whom I shall think of affectionately to the end of my days. The richness of this experience was due to many things. In such a community the spirit of a great tradi-tion has a potency of its own. But whatever was given out of a great inheritance, I am in no doubt that the ministry of the Rector — Monsignor Cormac Murphy-O'Connor[2] — was a key to the spirit of the College in my experience of it. The students varied in age and there were as many diversities of

[2]Monsignor Murphy-O'Connor was consecrated as Bishop of Arundel and Brighton in December 1977.

temperament and opinions as are to be found in any collegiate community: but two features common to them all made a deep impression on me.

First the tremendous personal appeal and inward hold on these men of their priestly vocation. The old seminary segregations have gone. Most of the external signs of the ordinands' setting-apart — habit and sometimes habits — are seldom apparent. In personal relationships, social life, and in a lively involvement in things contemporary, they were children of their time. Yet this coexisted with a profound sense of being set apart for the most tremendous and awe-inspiring responsibility that God was entrusting to them — an eternal, not merely temporal calling.

Some expressions of this as I met them were, of course, inseparable from distinctive features of Roman Catholic doctrine and practice — the meaning of ordination and ministry, the mystery of the Mass and the nature of priestly authority. Yet even deeper and more intimately personal than these things, I was aware again and again of the strength of a vocation which sees that of all mankind's needs, the most persistent, terrible, and demanding is that which springs from the inescapable fact of sin, and the need for forgiveness and redemption. This, first and last, is what a priestly ministry is about. Recognizing fundamental differences between 'Catholic' and 'Protestant' understandings of the means of grace, and of the Church's role in dealing with the mystery of iniquity, here lies the heart of all our callings to the ministry and the cure of souls.

Historically the Reformed ministry has been just as keenly aware of this, though I had lately feared that it was losing its pre-eminent place in a radical Christianity which does not always seem to be aware how deep are the roots of human nature. Living in a community unswervingly centred on it, I found myself challenged in a manner which recalled my first glimmerings of vocation to the Christian ministry, and the realization that this strange calling lies on a frontier between heaven and hell.

My second powerful impression is closely related to this. It concerns the priority given by these students to the life of prayer, the centrality of worship, and the recognition of the life-and-death necessity for the minister to nourish his own inner life at the springs of grace. This found expression in the ordered life of the community, with daily rendezvous before the altar and the disciplined study of the Bible and the classics of the spiritual life. What moved me chiefly in this was not the presence of external disciplines (these were of the slightest) but the utter naturalness and eagerness with which these men — and their women colleagues in the active, no less than the contemplative orders — sought the means of grace, talked about the life of the spirit, and took for granted its absolute priority.

I recognize some crucial differences between 'Protestant' and 'Catholic' understandings of 'spirituality', and I cannot ignore the challenge of the most radical contemporary questioning of many traditional assumptions and practices of the 'spiritual' life. But, again, I recall that the Reformed conception of the minister as a 'man of God' has included historically an unashamed assumption that amidst his greatest activities and most outgoing 'identification' with things temporal, he lives a life manifestly nurtured on things eternal. His ministry stands or falls by this.

A year after this memorable experience I was again in Rome as the guest of the English College. Fortuitously and most happily for me, my stay coincided with the ceremonies and celebrations associated with the Pope's recent creation of twenty new cardinals. These included Dom Basil Hume, recently elected Archbishop of Westminster, whose appointment had evoked in England not only the spontaneous good will of all the Churches, but the expectation of a distinctive contribution to the spiritual leadership of Britain at a time when that elusive but unmistakable quality — a new spirit — was so obviously needed. I was present in the Pope's Audience Hall at the imposition of birettas and titles upon the newly elevated cardinals. It was a colourful and jubilant affair, more like a popular festival than I had anticipated. The excitement, clapping, and cheering by the national supporters of the new dignitaries almost rivalled a cup-final, and the famous choir of the Sistine Chapel, not lacking in some piercing tones, was scarcely audible above the hubbub. When the Pope appeared, borne aloft in his ceremonial chair, the vociferous applause was deafening. Having innocently associated Roman ceremonial with notions of dignity which would shame the happy-go-lucky behaviour of some Protestant gatherings, I

143

was a bit startled. But I gradually became aware of the significance of this unexpected free-for-all. Indeed, before the
ceremony ended it would scarcely have seemed out of place
to me if the new cardinals — physically diminished in size by
the tremendous proportions of St Peter's and looking somewhat like schoolboys dragooned by the Master of Ceremonies
— had been presented not only with their birettas and parch-
ments but with a bag of buns and oranges. It was evidently
an occasion for high spirits in the Spirit. A few days later I
was in St Peter's when the Pope celebrated mass and all the
new cardinals concelebrated. Although there was again some
popular applause, the liturgy was attuned throughout to the
great notes of Christian worship, and I found it very moving,
not least because of a thread of simplicity which seemed to
run gently through the grandeur.

It may seem strange that in the light of all that I have said
in this chapter my Roman pilgrimage has not brought me any
nearer to the point of becoming a convert and 'making my
submission' to Rome. In any case I could not conceive a
change of ecclesiastical allegiance in terms of a 'submission'
except a new submission to the love of God in Christ — a submission that is required on every new morning. Any such
ecclesiastical change would have to be a jubilant leap into
some new dimension of the glorious liberty of the children of
God. Of course, as I hope I have clearly testified, I have long
since joyfully abandoned inherited distortions in the image of
the Roman Catholic Church. I have eagerly received correct-
ions and have been thankfully drawn into a clearer perception
and more humble acknowledgement of the immeasurable
riches of catholicity as Rome understands this word. Yet I
remain aware of the persistence of many of the historic differences which divide us doctrinally and ecclesiastically, and
which cannot be by-passed or ignored. The important con-
sensus statements on Baptism, Ministry, and the Eucharist,
which have been a highly significant product of ecumenical
discussion in recent years, have impressed me with the promise
of new depths of agreement still to come. But the goal is not
yet in sight. This applies still more to such questions as the
nature of authority in the Church and the role of the Pope.
Again, I now have more understanding and spiritual sympathy
with all that the role of the Virgin Mary means in Roman

Catholic spirituality. I have been helped towards this by such explanations and rationalizations as those which interpret the role of Mary as symbolizing the role of the Church in her docility to grace. I have appreciated the parallel between the Roman Catholic recourse to Mary's mediatorial work and the Protestant reliance on the 'advocacy' of the Holy Spirit. Yet I still cannot with full integrity of mind and heart sing hymns to the Virgin Mary despite the fact that I succumbed daily to the music of them in the Chapel of the Venerabile. Most poignantly nothing that I have yet been privileged to experience in my Roman pilgrimage has made it possible for me to receive communion in the course of the Roman mass, though all my heart has been in the splendour and power of the liturgy. This deprivation, felt most acutely within the depth of the unity I was experiencing at the Venerabile, was not due to lack of charity or good will on anybody's part but to issues which ultimately touch the integrity of our discipleship. For the Roman Catholic Church participation in the Eucharist is normally restricted to those who are Catholics and who have therefore explicitly accepted the Church's doctrine of the Sacrament. Certain exceptions to this are permissible but the Vatican requires that these must be 'confined to those who have a faith in the Sacrament in conformity with that of the Catholic Church and . . . for a long period are unable to have recourse to a minister of their own Communion.[3] Clearly I could not fulfil the second part of this requirement since there are Protestant churches in Rome with which I am in full communion and where I was able to receive the bread and wine. I was thus not deprived of the Sacrament; my deprivation was the inability to receive it in company with my new and dear Roman friends. But further, Rome would not regard my theology of the Sacrament as being 'in conformity with that of the Roman Catholic Church', even though I affirm with all my heart that through grace I experience the presence of Christ in the act of communion. It is well known, of course, that many Catholic priests do not apply these requirements in strict

[3] This wording is taken from an *Instruction Concerning Particular Cases when other Christians may be admitted to Eucharistic Communion* issued in 1973 by the Vatican Secretariat for Unity.

obedience to the letter of them. In many parts of the world, in fact, there is an increasing disregard of the regulations. But I was in Rome, the privileged guest of a 'pontifical' community, and I had no right to ask or expect my hosts to be indifferent to the rules governing their office. Much as I longed to communicate, that courtesy which I believe to be a derivative of grace would have been sufficient to prevent my asking. I must also add that for me communion by concession rather than conviction is unsatisfactory. Hard as it is to withhold, I would rather wait until we have reached a common conviction that at Christ's table we are all equally subjects of his amazing concession and therefore dispense the sacraments and receive them as those who have no status in the matter other than that of penitents who gratefully adore the Lord whose table it is. In Rome I could not by-pass these differences or expect others to do so, and I was left in no doubt that my new friends felt this grievous flaw in the corporate expression of our unity as searchingly as I did. Nevertheless, as I ventured to say in the College chapel, if we accept the obligation to 'share the pain of our separation', we must make speedier progress in ending the separation lest we drift into a kind of morbid indulgence which is in fact giving pain to our Lord more than it is hurting ourselves or one another.

I must reckon with the possibility that so long as I thankfully apprehend the authentic riches of Roman Catholicism but stop short of committing myself to its claims, I am being held back only because I still insist on routing my Roman pilgrimage via Geneva (I speak in parables). In that city of Calvin and the Reformation there is a massive Reformation monument carved out against a formidable wall, and I admit that I have never tried to scale the wall. Yet I have never sojourned for long in Geneva at the Reformation monument. I have always spent far more time at the Ecumenical Centre. And it is at this location (still speaking in parables) that I can best express the greatest thing that my Roman pilgrimage has done for me. With my Roman Catholic friends I found that even at points where, in respect of doctrine and ecclesiology, I had to say 'I cannot accept this', I knew without a shadow of doubt that at the greatest of all spiritual depths we belonged to one another in the confidence that we were on pilgrimage with each other and with a Lord who is leading us into a fuller understanding of the term 'one holy catholic and apostolic Church' than any of us has yet perceived or experienced.

I am not sure whether my Roman pilgrimage has made me a Catholic Protestant or a Protestant Catholic. I hope it has made me a better Christian. If it has, it is because through all the privileges I have acknowledged in this chapter I have learned more of the grace which is heart-breaking and heart-mending and through which we have all been made blood-brothers at the cross of Christ.

9 *I BELIEVE . . .*

'How can you hold on to the Faith in view of all that we have lived through?' This question has often been put to me and it is a *cri de coeur* as old as the hills. 'If the Lord be with us,' cried Gideon, 'why then hath all this befallen us and where be all his mighty works which our fathers told us of?'

In the agelong succession of those who have wrestled with this question I have had to confess that I have not held on to the faith; the faith has held on to me. At times the grip seems to have loosened or I have slipped out of its grasp, or even tried to wriggle out. Yet I remain held by it and I am thankful beyond words. Can I say how this hold has been exercised? Not completely, for the explanation lies deeper than reason — above reason I am convinced, not below it. The most I can do is to try to say in what discernible ways life has compelled me and still compels me to say, 'I believe'.

'I believe' is an individual and personal affirmation. When the affirmation is made with a warmth and strength that involves the whole person and makes *Credo* a great musical assertion, it implies that faith has become a very personal affair. This is so for me. Yet I cannot detach my personal confession of faith from a whole network of relationships with other men and women. All that is contained in the preceding chapters of this book illustrates this. In the nature of the case, the most powerful influences in bringing me to the experience of faith and sustaining me in it have come through men and women whom I have known and lived with, worked with, and worshipped with. Yet I have always been aware that these visible relationships have been part of a wider complex of involvements and dependencies which link me with believers whom I have never known in the flesh. These are the faithful of other generations, those who have left on record their own testimony to the validity of the Christian revelation, recording events, offering their reflections upon the events, and living their lives in the light of their own Christian experience and convictions. I am debtor to this past and heir to it. In a characteristic

148

comment on some of the symptoms of what we should now call 'the generation gap', G.K. Chesterton once remarked that when we are confronted with, or affronted by what appears to be the boorish behaviour of the young, 'it is not enough to say, "Your Uncle Hiram was deeply shocked", or "What your Great-Aunt Abigail would have thought I cannot imagine",' for the young man is left with the impression that he is merely getting on the wrong side of Uncle Hiram, whereas he is 'getting on the wrong side of Socrates and Confucius, and Dante and Shakespeare, and the whole cumulative culture and ordered imagination of mankind. We must not only tell him sharply to mend his manners, or even to mind his manners. We must tell him to mind his mind.'[1]

We cannot, of course, live by the example of the past, and we certainly cannot believe simply because earlier generations have done so. It has evidently proved easier for me to be held by the faith because of the convincing character of my Christian inheritance and upbringing. But this does not happen automatically or invariably. The deportment of Chesterton's Aunt Abigail and Uncle Hiram has been the provoking cause of revolt rather than imitation, and it is notorious that a godly upbringing has resulted in making it more difficult for many men and women to adopt the faith of their fathers. Nevertheless, granted the gift of a personal and contemporary experience leading to the 'I believe', then the relation of this experience to the whole of Christian history becomes a source of immeasurable encouragement, reassurance, and strength. It is no small thing to be on the right side of the apostles, of the authors of the Gospels, of Augustine and Dante and Milton, of Luther and Wesley and Richard Baxter and William Penn and Isaac Watts — not forgetting John Sebastian Bach.

This is simply to say that I believe in the Church and that I have been held by the Christian faith very largely within the fellowship of believers. This at once touches on one of the many paradoxes of the Christian life, for the Church is repellant as well as attractive. I recall that in my student days, when I was beginning to read Bright's *Age of the Fathers* a friend said to me: 'You need to have been soundly converted

[1] G.K. Chesterton, *Sidelights.*

to stomach the reading of Church history without plumping for atheism.' This was putting it rather strongly but I soon discovered the reason for the comment. I believe that the Councils of Nicaea and Chalcedon were concerned with an issue central to our understanding of God, life, and destiny. And I acknowledge that they finally testified to the truth of the matter. Yet had I been at either of these assemblies I fear that I should have been sadly put off by the temper and conduct of some of the protagonists. I am the more dismayed by this realization because I know full well that Nicaea and Chalcedon were not the only or the last occasions on which the Church in its assemblies has disgraced itself through the behaviour of its members. I have participated in too many assemblies, committees, and other gatherings of professed Christians to be ignorant of this. This does not mean that I can be complacent about the phenomenon. I remain mystified and troubled. The mystery deepens when I recall that we have to go further back into history than the age of the Fathers to perceive the first signs of this malady. Jesus had 'set his face towards Jerusalem', where he was to demonstrate the meaning of divinity by taking on him the form of a servant and becoming obedient unto death. On that occasion, we read, the disciples followed and were afraid, and on their uncertain road 'there began a dispute amongst them which of them would be greatest'. In face of the final self-giving of their Master those who were closest to him could be self-seeking and quarrelsome over a matter of prestige. Church history, continuing to our own time, bears witness to a lamentable historic succession of defaulters in the realm of Christian behaviour.

It is only by going back as far as this that I can come to terms with the shame of the Church. That quarrel on the road to Jerusalem was not the last word. Even in face of those dark hours when all forsook him and fled and one denied him and another betrayed him, there is more to be said about the glorious company of the apostles. This is true of the whole course of the history of the Church. It has been a fellowship of forgiveness as well as an arena in which many have stumbled. It has been a community in which betrayals have been transcended by heroic obediences, where sin has been redeemed and where countless men and women have proved to be holy and humble of heart through the grace which makes, sustains, and constantly renews the fellowship of Christ's people.

From this standpoint I think of the shocks and disappointments I have experienced in my long membership of the Church — the gloomy or bombastic seniors whose deportment frightened and baffled me in childhood, the pompous little office-bearers, the vain parsons and futile preachers, and pillars of the church who were patently not monuments to goodness and mercy outside the church. If I could weep at some of these poor witnesses I can also marvel at what Christ did with them and, far exceeding their number, I think of the great multitude whose lives have adorned the doctrine, portrayed the splendour of the Christian life, and have proved to be authentic witnesses of the resurrection. When I am most saddened by the failure of the Church, I remember William Penn's word, 'They have a right to censure who have a heart to help'. Further, and most important of all for my understanding of the Church and the ways of its Lord, whenever I feel that Christ is saying again to the community of his disciples, 'One of you shall betray me', rather than looking around the table for the potential delinquents I can only say, 'Lord, is it I?' I believe in the Church.

What Church? Which Church out of the many separated institutions? Because of my father's conversion, I was baptized and nurtured in Methodism — that part of it which was then known as Wesleyan Methodism. I have never lost my sense of gratitude to Methodism, even though the first Methodist minister in whom I confided my thoughts about possibly becoming a minister scouted the notion and I did not dare to speak about it to him again. The family's removal to another district was the main non-theological cause for our becoming Congregationalists. My best growing years in the faith, my love for the Church, and my ordination to the Christian ministry are bound up with this Church, now united with Presbyterianism in the United Reformed Church.[2]

[2] Amongst other opportunities with which I have been favoured in my ministry have been the Chairmanship of the Congregational Union of England and Wales (1954), the Moderatorship of the International Congregational Council (1962-6), and the Moderatorship of the Free Church Federal Council (1966-7).

At the heart of historic Congregationalism or Independency there is a doctrine of the Church which affirms that the local 'gathered' congregation of committed believers in which the Word is faithfully preached and the sacraments administered, and whose members corporately seek to be ruled by that Holy Spirit which is the living Christ, constitutes a focal point or outcrop of the Church universal. I still assent to this belief. I have, however, long since had to ask 'What are the marks of the Church universal which should be apparent in this local outcrop if the claim is to prove valid?' Local independence must not become a local insularity which ignores the world-wide interdependence of gathered congregations. The claim of the local church to exercise an authority inherent in it by its subjection to the Spirit's guidance needs to be balanced by recognition of the authority bestowed by the same Spirit on the Church in its more than local gatherings. Hence the integrity of the local congregation requires an openness to the guidance, the correctives, and the experience of the Church universal. Here my commitment to the ecumenical movement has proved vital for my own local churchmanship as well as for my understanding of the nature and calling of the universal Church. To have been privileged to know the people and be involved in the events which I have already recorded has been a liberal education in the ways of grace. It has also made me dissatisfied with any local church which is content to remain a 'denomination' instead of constantly seeking to become a manifest expression of the one holy catholic and apostolic Church. In terms of personal relationships, rapport of mind and heart, and unity in the Spirit I belong as deeply to other Churches as to my own. Yet there is no adequate correspondence between this sense of belonging and my accepted membership and ministry in many other communions. The most acute symptom of this is at that point where it would be most natural, as it is deeply needed, to be openly together at the table of the Lord. The term 'separated brethren' has had an interesting development in its usage during my lifetime. At first the emphasis was on 'separated'. This was in the main the Anglican attitude to Free Churchmen and the Roman Catholic attitude to Anglicans, Free Churchmen, and all others. Gradually the emphasis shifted from 'separated' to 'brethren'. Within the experiences and graces of ecumenical relationships there has in recent years been a growing recognition that we are all brethren and all sadly separated, and that so long as the separations continue we are all impoverished in our knowledge of the gospel, our understanding of the Church, and our appropriation of the fullness of grace. This is not admitted by all, of course, but it is a truth which lies at the heart of what I believe the ecumenical movement implies. In my experience commitment to the movement brings home this truth most searchingly and it provides the incentive towards making the movement move, until we all come to the unity of the faith and the knowledge of the Son of God. It is this fellowship of believers in process of becoming, this Church still *in via*, in which I believe and to which, by the mercy of God, I belong.

What of the gospel that has laid hold of me, that gospel which creates and sustains the Church and is its proclamation to the world? When I entered the Christian ministry in the immediate aftermath of the First World War, I was still held by what I understood to be that Gospel of the Kingdom which must first be preached to all nations. This denoted the acknowledged rule of God over all life, over all human behaviour and relationships, an assured reign which is good news about the purpose of God in creation and for mankind. Within this accomplished reign of God there would be an end to sin and suffering, injustice, and all other wrongs. In the words of an Old Testament prophecy with which Jesus began his ministry, this gospel of the Kingdom promises release to the captives, the setting at liberty of those who are oppressed, and good news for the poor. As I and most of my generation recognized, acceptance of this good news about the purpose of life involved commitment to all those causes which seek to realize these goals and make the world a better place. To be a Christian was to be a crusader for these ends. Our lives were to be dedicated towards ensuring that there would be no more war, that the causes of war — economic and political — would be removed, and that an international society based on justice and freedom would be realized on earth. We believed that there would be greater fulfilment of these ideals in that fuller life of the Kingdom which lies beyond time and space, but in the meantime we were crusaders led by the pioneer and captain of our faith, fighting for those

Christian values and relationships which would turn the world upside down, or right side up. 'These things shall be!' we sang:

> . . . A loftier race
> Than e'er the world hath known, shall rise
> With flame of freedom in their souls
> And light of knowledge in their eyes.

We recognized that this better warfare of the Kingdom must make searching demands on us in the way we live and the use of our time and resources, and in our understanding of the meaning of life. But all these demands and disciplines were seen to be part of God's good news for us. There was a purpose in living. As Bernard Shaw wrote in *Man and Superman*, 'This is the true joy in life, the being used for a purpose recognized by yourself as a mighty one, the being thoroughly worn out before you are thrown on the scrap-heap, the being a force of Nature instead of a feverish, selfish little clod of ailments and grievances complaining that the world will not devote itself to making you happy.' Shaw's ideal of becoming a force of Nature, or one with the Life Force, was scarcely the equivalent of obedience to the will of the God and Father of our Lord Jesus Christ. Nevertheless Shaw knew that the need for a way of life which will deliver us from aimlessness is something which belongs to our nature. Today the areas of human need in which the Christian is called to find life through a crusading obedience to a radical Christianity are greater and more clamorous than ever. Recognition of this remains for me an imperative of the gospel.

Yet I believe that to stop here is to stop short of apprehending that which is most central to the meaning of Christianity. Because traditional Christian language has for many people lost its savour, there has of late been a tendency to substitute the world 'liberation' for 'salvation'. For millions in our day liberation is, of course, a good-news word in what it promises to the victims of tyranny and injustice and in the costly crusading which it demands from those with the power to help. Liberation speaks with a saving accent. But liberation from what and to what?

Within the total mystery of our existence there are two areas in which I am most conscious of the depth of our need and the power of the gospel. These are both areas in which we need liberation in its profoundest saving significance. The first is the mystery of evil and the second the mystery of death.

I am not a professional theologian and I lack the technical equipment to be one. Yet I have never been willing to separate theology and experience. Such experience of the reality and power of the gospel as has been given to me is inseparable from what I have learned in the study of theology and I can think of no higher calling, nor one more essential to the future of the Church and the fulfilment of its mission than that of the theologian. Yet it is not as such that I write. I am here simply trying to say how certain convictions have taken hold on me and maintained their hold. If my testimony is true, of course it carries with it considerable theological implications.

I suppose I have never been able to exclude from my own pilgrimage of faith the realization of what I owe to the original conversion of my father. No doubt I could have become disillusioned or sceptical about this, as others have done with a similar inheritance. I could have regarded it as a dated phenomenon or explained it away. This I have never been able to do. I know, with a knowledge 'felt in the blood and felt along the heart' that from New Testament times to this present year of grace the most distinctive thing about Christianity is its power to effect radical changes, changes in the course of history, changes in a man's way of life, changes in human nature.

The struggle to achieve a better life for all men must go on, through political and economic liberation, through the ending of discrimination on grounds of race or sex, through the abolition of war and the treatment of its causes. But that question which Martin Buber addressed to me is still writ large across the world today. 'Is there any power in the universe which can deal with the intractable heart of man?' Buber knew that the problem is not simply the intractable hearts of individual men and women. It is the even more hard-hearted condition of intractable societies, of man in his corporate ability to impede good and let evil have its way. 'These things shall be! A loftier race . . . shall rise . . .' But how? And why do those lines now ring so hollow and sound so juvenile? Why does it now seem so incongruous that when they were most widely sung in the nineteen-twenties they were innocently set to a Welsh tune called 'Dies Irae'?[3]

We do not get the full measure of the mystery of evil, nor do we appraise our predicament adequately if we think solely in terms of the individual's need for conversion or of society's need for reform. True, the gospel speaks to both these needs. It contains power to convert the individual and it calls to a way of life derived from the example and precepts of Jesus which challenge the bases and assumptions of contemporary society. Yet evil does not disappear in the presence of a number of converted individuals, nor does progress towards a more just social order destroy its power, even though the occasions for its operation may be reduced. The most truly converted Christian, living a life of sanctity, knows that he has not attained and that his 'good' life is poised on a razor edge. 'Let him that thinketh he standeth take heed lest he fall.' Both the good man and the just society are always threatened by the corrosive and corrupting power of evil.

There is no explanation of the origin of evil. Many evils can of course be traced to particular causes and remedies found for them, but this does not touch the real heart of the problem. At that mysterious core there is a baffling and unanswerable question. This question is only part of the everlasting Why which arises from many other aspects of one experience. There is that strange element of contingency running through so much of life, the chance event which suddenly transforms a situation or life, the untimely happenings which defy rhyme or reason and, supremely, the final contingency of death. Nowhere does this contingent element raise more anguished questions than when a life of great achievement or promise is smitten with paralysis or some incurable disease, or cut off at the most untimely moment. One of the most eloquent responses to this everlasting Why recorded in the Bible is that of Job's three friends when they first arrived at the house of desolation. 'They sat down with him upon the

[3] The words of this hymn were taken from a poem of John Addington Symonds called 'A Vista', published in 1880. It was later adopted by the old League of Nations Union and much used in leaflet form at meetings of the Union in the nineteen-twenties.

ground seven days and seven nights and not one spake a word unto him for they saw that his grief was very great.' It is true that if a week later they had not then embarked upon their multitude of words subsequent ages would have been deprived of some of the greatest and most moving poetry ever written. It would be a pity if we had to do without even the impertinent eloquence of the young upstart Elihu who, having listened with growing impatience to his elders, threw in his masterly maiden speech with the excuse that 'great men are not always wise, neither do the aged understand'. But Job's verdict on his sick-visitors' magnificent volubility was right. 'Miserable comforters are ye all. Shall vain words have an end?' If these good folk, old or young, had realized the kind of comfort which alone could speak to Job's condition they would have left quietly after the first week.

When Gideon voiced his version of the everlasting Why we are told that he addressed it to an angel. What was the reply? Not an answer but a command. 'Go in this thy strength . . . thou mighty man of valour.' At that point Gideon was feeling far from strong and anything but valiant. If his question remained unanswered his need as a man in face of misfortune was amply met. 'The Lord looked upon him and said, . . . 'Surely I will be with thee.' So Gideon then built an altar.

It is at another place of sacrifice that faith holds me fast in face of the mystery of evil and contingency and that last enemy death. I know what it was that happened to Bunyan's pilgrim when he came to 'a place somewhat ascending. Upon that place stood a cross and a little below an open sepulchre . . . . Then I saw in my dream that just as Christian came up with the cross his burden loosed off his shoulders and fell from off his back and began to tumble till it came to the mouth of the sepulchre where it fell in and I saw it no more . . . . Then was Christian glad and lightsome and said with a merry heart, "He hath given me rest by his sorrow and life by his death".' For Bunyan in his pilgrimage the burden was the excessive burden of sin, that strange manifestation of evil in the wayward heart of man when we have to admit that we do the wrong things even against our own will. Here is the sting not only of death but of life. It is good that in our own time we have learned to make more merciful discriminations than hitherto between sin and guilt, and that even some of the more revolting behaviour of disordered men and women is now diagnosed with the tolerant and less emotional re-action of physicians treating disease. But the root of the problem remains. 'The good that I would I do not; the evil that I would not, that I do.' But the burden on the shoulders of the pilgrim named Everyman is compounded not only of sin but of all the heartache caused by anxiety and fear, not least by the fear that in our own time 'progress' has brought us to the point where our sophisticated societies are on the verge of becoming cities of destruction and cities of dreadful night.

How is it that at the cross of Christ such a burden can be shifted from shoulders that cannot bear it? I cannot say how. I can only say Who it is who lifts it. There is a sense in which the cross of Christ can be regarded as the type and essence of all other crosses. Jesus was not the first or the last man to be deserted and betrayed by his friends, unfairly condemned, executed by singularly cruel means and dying with forgive-ness on his lips. The story of mankind has been made all the nobler because so many men and women have proved to be as good as this. I have frequently used the word 'mystery' in relation to evil. It is no less applicable to what we call good-ness and to the fact that by some deep immemorial instinct we can make this discrimination between evil and goodness, a discriminating power which remains profoundly significant wherever the line has been drawn in varying ethical and cultural situations. On the cross of Christ there is portrayed this mystery of goodness shining above the darkness of the evil which occasioned it. Here is the light which shines in the darkness and the darkness cannot overcome it.

Yet while this is part of the power of the cross of Christ it is not the whole. The mystery of goodness embodied in Jesus is bound up with the greater mystery of his person. Of all the good men and women who have lived and died sacrificially and forgivingly none has transformed other men's natures as he has done, nor evoked so powerful a conviction that in his presence, supremely in the manner and aftermath of his death, we are in the presence of God himself. He was man, genuine man. He represents all that we ought to be if we are to be whole, fully integrated as persons. Yet he embodies in himself that which is more than human nature and which becomes our judgement as well as our hope. 'Never man spake like this man.' This was not a comment on his oratory; it was a confession that through his words human nature was being moved by a power and grace that is more than human. 'He spake with authority.' Not simply with greater force or expertise; it was the power of ultimate truth communicating itself through his person. He healed diseases and cast out devils, not as a faith healer or dealer in formulae for exorcism but by the presence within him and proceeding from him of that spirit of wholeness which is the Holy Spirit of God. The miracles are not proofs of his more than human nature, but being what he was, who he was, it is not surprising that he gave evidence of moving in the world of nature as one who was *en rapport* with the secret of its ways. In his death he endured the worst that evil can do, and in his broken body he was one with our mortality. But though the mystery of his resurrection baffled the capacity of its various witnesses to describe it with full consistency, of one thing they were unswervingly agreed. Contrary to their expectation and beyond their hope they could now say 'Christ is risen!' God was in Christ.

God was in Christ. In this assertion by successive generations of Christians there is the one continuous thread within the long and chequered story of the Church, the people of Christ. When I make this same conviction my own, as most thankfully and wonderingly I do, I am not simply saying that God was present in Christ in the sense that his presence is discernible in the lives of other men and women. I am declaring my conviction that in the person of Jesus Christ there was an authentic disclosure of what lies at the heart of the mystery that we call God. Further, I make this assertion not only in the past tense, though the historic event is crucial, the once upon a time disclosure opens my eyes and heart to the reality and contemporary activity of a Christ-like God. I do not thereby know everything that is to be known in this life or beyond this life of the nature of God as the ultimate source, meaning, and purpose of life. All that we in our finitude postulate when we use the word 'God' remains a mystery. But in the light of Jesus Christ it becomes a mystery with a luminous centre. From this luminous centre there shines light upon life, there flows power for right living, there is communicated truth in an aliveness which evokes conviction and creates faith. Many of the questions which are part of the everlasting Why remain unanswered, and I dare not try to check the urgent probings of my mind; I cannot narcotize reason. The life of faith, as I understand this through Christ, does not atrophy any of my senses. Rather it quickens them and stirs more readily and profoundly the emotions accompanying all sensual experience. Beauty is more deliriously exciting, happiness more exuberant, pain more acute, and sorrow more sorrowful; hurts in love are more heart-breaking and love's healings more heart-mending. I cry more easily and laugh more readily. The reaction of my senses as well as my reason to the sin and sorrow of the world is the more touched with anguish when, at the cross of Christ, I hear his 'My God, my God, why . . . ?' Yet perceiving there and at the empty tomb who he is I know that he enables even me to say 'Into thy hands . . .'

These are the hands into which I have learned through Christ to put my trust. I believe they are the hands which have led me into the experiences and relationships which I have tried faithfully to record in this book. They have not let me go even when I have thought life would be easier if I could be released from their grasp. They have been there when I have felt their hold was loosening and when, in some sickness of the soul, I have harboured the poison of unforgivingness and not wished for an antidote. They have held me at places of insistent and baffled questioning. They have brought me to viewpoints where I have seen more clearly my immeasurable debt to others, my own terrible undeservingness, my debt of honour to serve and go on serving if I am really to live and not merely exist. From those hands I have received in worship the bread of life and the wine of life and in faith, hope, and love I believe they are the hands which will guide me through death unto the life that is life indeed.

I do not make this affirmation lightly or on the assumption that even for a Christian the final act of dying must assuredly be accompanied by a consciousness of peace at the last. It happens that after writing a first draft of this chapter I was subject to major surgical treatment. The operation was successful but some time later I suffered a pulmonary

embolism. Strangely enough, during this I regained consciousness for a few seconds (or a split second, I do not know
which) and in that interval I was agonizingly aware of the
struggle for breath. Its desperate character was such that (as
I was later told) in another gasp or two I should have 'gone'.
In the midst of the agony and on the brink of death all capacity for thought and for any willed act of faith were
completely absent. I was only a piece of flesh struggling to
stay alive. Were the everlasting arms no longer under me or
the receiving hands withdrawn? I find it impossible to believe
this, any more than I can doubt that the prayers of the saints,
on earth and in heaven, were encompassing me. I cannot say
how grace operates on a mind paralysed by pain or upon a
soul wracked by the death struggle of this body of our
humiliation. Maybe, as someone has said, 'God does not give
dying grace to live with, but he will be there when the time
comes.' So I believe; and having been given grace to live with
for a little longer it is for me unthinkable that his hands,
compassionate and redeeming, were not there in my agony or
would not have held me fast if another gasp had ended my
sojourn in this world. In life or death, I believe.

I have so far indulged in a very personal affirmation of
belief and trust. Some might regard it as too individualistic,
a private faith tending to escapism. Can I go further and say
with equal confidence that the hands into which I put my
trust belong to one who 'has the whole world in his hands'?
Is the remedy for the mess and pain of things in his hands?
Will it come right in the end? If I no longer sing with the
optimism of sixty years ago 'These things shall be . . .', have
I now changed to 'These things shall not be', and language
more appropriately set to a *Dies irae*?

The faith by which I am held falsifies many expectations
of a 'better world'. Facts as well as faith have shattered many
illusions which were once thought to be attainable ideals. The
title of C.E. Montague's novel of the early 'twenties —
Disenchantment — has been writ large over the history of the
last fifty years. The hopes we cherished in my young days
were worthy and not to be despised. They were hopes of a
world refashioned in the light of the Kingdom of God. But
our notions of the character of that Kingdom and the way to
it were too facile. It required a more radical revolution than

161

we had contemplated and this demanded not only a more realistic recognition of the power of evil; it called for acceptance of a scale of values, of the purpose of life as Christ has revealed it, which must run counter to most of the goals which the natural man makes the measure of success, prosperity, happiness, and peace. The acquisitive society is not a prefiguring of the Kingdom of God. It is a disfiguring. The affluent society can be poverty-stricken in the everlasting values of life. The permissive society can become a society enslaved by destructive desires. So long as the motivations which appear to determine the main course of 'civilization' continue to be the dominant aim of society, the coming of a fundamentally better world is a dubious hope.

But what relation has a better world to the Kingdom of God? I have recalled some of the hopes and determinations with which many of my generation entered upon the Christian ministry in the nineteen-twenties. There was clearly a certain innocence about some of our assumptions. In the immediate aftermath of the First World War — that 'war to end war' — it was easy to say 'Never again', and to believe that a second such tragedy was unthinkable. It is a long way from that innocence to the state of mind in which further and more terribly destructive wars, even to the point of a possible extinction of human life, have become complacently thinkable. Yet with all our innocence fifty years ago and the inevitability of more terrible awakenings, at least we did not limit the horizons of our hope to this world. We believed that every step towards the betterment of life through greater justice and charity, through reducing the gap between the haves and the have-nots and the promotion of peace between nations and races could provide some foretaste of the meaning of the Kingdom of God.

I still believe that there is continuity between God's purpose for life in this world and the nature of his eternal Kingdom. What we do here, individually and corporately, is vitally related to our apprehension and enjoyment of a state of existence in which good has finally triumphed over evil and the purpose of our creation has reached a glorious consummation. When our days here are lived to the full and in keeping with the mind and spirit of Jesus Christ we can experience in foretaste some degree of what is meant by the

Kingdom of God in which life is no longer threatened by evil or frustration and is not terminable by death. But I think that the relation between these foretastes of the Kingdom in the here and now and their completed realization in the 'beyond' is something which has to be understood in terms that are more than chronological. Of necessity I am here moving into deep and uncharted waters. We live within the dimension of time and the coming and going of hours, weeks, months, and years is part of the nature of our existence, the reality with which we have to reckon. Since the time-space dimension is so fundamental to all our thinking, experiencing, knowing, and being, we can only assume that it is vitally related to our continued growth in all that awaits us after death. Nevertheless even within this time-scene there are experiences common to us all which are not wholly measurable or explainable in terms of hours or years. *I never noticed the time. It seemed only yesterday. Time sped. Time dragged. It was glorious out of all proportion to the time it lasted. It seemed as though time stood still and no longer mattered. I lost count of time. It was a heavenly experience.* Perhaps the common and instinctive use of the word 'heavenly' in this connection has more than a casual significance. We are capable of heavenly experiences on earth. Even when they are most fleeting in time they possess a quality which makes them more than transient. They have their own power of communicating something indestructible. They become part of our lives from their 'moment' onwards. Henceforth we do not only remember them; we recollect them and appropriate their grace afresh.

I believe this is meant to be more than the private experience of an individual. There are corporate achievements and realizations which possess this same power of transcending time and becoming part of a reality which is not finally conditioned by years. For example, I have known this within the meaning of a rich family life. With all its imperfections, mistakes, and struggles, I know that the family can be a set of relationships rooted and held together by something more than biological ties. Within it there are loyalties, acknowledged dependencies and commitments, shared experiences of joy and sorrow, companionships to the gates of death, which become the vehicle of a fellowship that is timeless. This is what such a conception as immortality and the communion of saints means to me. These mysteries do not simply imply that after death there will be continuities which go on in endless 'time'. If indeed time were their framework, a primary concomitant of their reality, some curious questions would arise. In the year when I write this my mother, had she survived on earth, would be 118 years old, my father 120. Those little brothers and sisters whose fleeting days ended long before I was born would mostly be in their nineties. Does immortality mean that after death I shall be re-introduced to all these in some celestial old people's home? I hope not. No, I am one with those now in unities which are neither old nor young, but timeless and ageless. With my present powers of apprehension I cannot tell what form this experienced unity will take after my death, but I cannot conceive of its being less real or satisfying than I know it to be now. For me it is a gospel inference that it will exceed the rich yet imperfect relationships I enjoy in time. I believe it will contain more wonders, fulfilments, and surprises, and that past and present experience will be subsumed and transcended in a greater Now. I hold fast to this assumption of faith when I think not only of those who have gone before us into the world of Light, but of my grandchildren and great-grandchildren whose dear lives time will fail me to witness in their fullness. To such mysteries as these, with their unknowable aspects in time, faith encourages me to apply the words: 'If it were not so I would have told you.'

It is my belief that this view of the relationship between life in these dimensions of time-space and life fulfilled as God intends it to be in his Kingdom, can be extended to all aspects of life in this world, supremely at all those points where the issue of good and evil is joined. No victory of good over evil is ever lost. No attempt to fashion life in greater accord with the mind of Christ is evanescent. Even within this time-scene the achievements of the seekers after truth, beauty, and right relationships transmit their imperishable legacy to subsequent generations. The humanist may be bravely content to limit the significance of these things to the time-span of history; all due honour to such. But I believe that in Christ there is better news than this.

Work done with integrity of mind and hand, the endeavour

to create a just society, the dedication of individuals and groups to the service of him who is the way, the truth, and the life — these things are part of life in the Kingdom of God; they are charged with those powers and graces of the Kingdom that are indestructible. In the light of this conviction working for a 'better world' is never a vain endeavour. Nor is it travailing for an earthly paradise, an ever-receding utopia. It is living now as citizens of that Kingdom which is illimitable in its possibilities and which will endure when the fashion of this world has passed away and time shall be no more.

All that I have here tried to express as my personal belief is bound up with what I have said about the Church whose witness, fellowship, and worship have been and are inseparable for my understanding of the faith and of faith's hold on me. I can make as many criticisms of the Church as can any of its onlookers; even more because of the nature of my lifelong involvement in it. Yet deeper than its imperfections and shortcomings, the Church remains for me the supreme expression of the fellowship of the Kingdom. Within its life I meet the imperatives of Christian discipleship, the constantly renewed summons to service and obedience. Within the Church I find that larger family life which transcends time and links me with all its members in heaven and on earth in a present unity which will become more complete beyond time. In the Church's worship, through its spiritual disciplines and means of grace, I know that evil cannot have the last word because there is a remedy for sin — my own and the world's. I know that death has been defeated by the kind of victory that turns enemies — even the last enemy — into friends. Believing all this and living in the strength of it, how can I order my life or contemplate my death without thanksgiving, or cease to want to tell the world why, in promise and not illusion, even in the darkest days young men may see visions and old men dream dreams of a Kingdom which cannot be shaken, a Kingdom of love, joy, peace. This is the Kingdom which surpasses even our heart's desire because it is the desire and will of the God and Father of our Lord Jesus Christ and our Father. It is this for which we pray 'Thy Kingdom come'. Amen; so be it!